FÉNELON

FRANCISCUS DE SALIGNAC VEL SALAGNAC DE LA MOTHE FENELON · ARCHIEPISCOPUS · DUX CAMERACENSIS

Princes que le Ciel a fait naistre,
Pour nous donner de justes Loix,
Choisissez ce Mentor pour Maistre
Il sceut l'art de former les Rois.

J. Vivien pinxit.   P. Drevet sculp.

FÉNELON

HIS LIFE AND WORKS

BY THE LATE
PAUL JANET

Translated and Edited with
Introduction, Notes, and Index

BY

VICTOR LEULIETTE

KENNIKAT PRESS
Port Washington, N. Y./London

FENELON

First published in 1914
Reissued in 1970 by Kennikat Press
Library of Congress Catalog Card No: 78-113315
ISBN 0-8046-0997-7

Manufactured by Taylor Publishing Company   Dallas, Texas

IN PIOUS AND AFFECTIONATE MEMORY

OF

WILLIAM EDWARD COLLINS, D.D.

LATE LORD BISHOP OF GIBRALTAR

AND

FORMERLY PROFESSOR OF ECCLESIASTICAL HISTORY

AT KING'S COLLEGE, LONDON

CONTENTS

INTRODUCTION

PAUL-ALEXANDRE-RENÉ JANET, philosopher, man of letters, moralist, and historian, was born in Paris on the 30th of April, 1823, of a family of booksellers, which, as he said, " n'avait rien à regretter de l'Ancien Régime." He entered the École Normale at the age of 18, where he formed lifelong friendships with Hippolyte Rigault, the critic, François Thurot, the philologist, and Émile Burnouf, the orientalist. In 1844, he passed the final examination, of which Victor Cousin, the chief examiner, says in his report : " Sa leçon sur la divine Providence est assurément une des plus fortes et des plus belles que j'aie entendues depuis quinze ans. La doctrine la plus pure, une méthode sévère, un rare savoir, une élocution nette et vigoureuse ont, pendant une heure entière, captivé un nombreux auditoire." The same year, Janet became private secretary to Cousin, and assiduously worked with him on his great edition of Pascal's *Pensées*. In 1845, he collaborated in Cousin's immortal work, *Du Vrai, du Beau, et du Bien*.

After a year spent in close intimacy with

INTRODUCTION

the founder of the modern Eclectic School of philosophy, Paul Janet was " affranchi de cette noble et sévère tutelle," by his appointment to the lectureship in moral philosophy at the Royal College of Bourges. In 1848, at the early age of 25, he was nominated to the Chair of Philosophy in the Faculty of Arts of Strasbourg University, where he remained for eight years. He had just obtained his Doctorate with two brilliant theses : the one, on the dialectics of Plato, which was subsequently published as an essay under the title of *Études sur la dialectique dans Platon et dans Hegel :* the other, in Latin, *De plastica naturæ vita quæ a Cudwortho in systemate intellectuali celebratur.* His chief friends at Strasbourg were his colleagues Jules Zeller, the historian of Germany and Italy, Michel Bréal, the philologist and grammarian, and Louis Pasteur, the chemist and bacteriologist ; to the latter, in particular, he owed his appreciation of the value of scientific methods in the investigation and exposition of psychological facts. In 1855, he delivered an eloquent and exceedingly well-attended series of public Lectures on *La Famille.* Published later in bookform, this fruitful and most attractive work was crowned by the French Academy in 1856 ; it has been translated into many languages, and is now in its thirteenth edition. From 1857 to 1863, he was Professor of Logic at the Lycée Louis-le-Grand, in Paris. In the latter year, his beautiful, optimistic, and powerful book entitled *La philosophie du Bonheur* was crowned by the Academy. On this occasion, Villemain, the reporter on the Prize-competitions of the year, wrote : "Ce n'est pas seulement au nom d'une philosophie généreuse qu'il combat la doctrine de La Rochefoucauld ; c'est du spectacle même de la vie qu'il fait ressortir la réprobation de l'égoïsme."

In 1864, Paul Janet was elected a member of the Academy of Moral and Political Sciences, in succession to Louis-René Villermé, the physician, statistician, and philanthropist. In June of the same year, he succeeded Émile Saisset as Professor of the History of Philosophy in Paris University, a post which he continued to fill with devotion and distinction for twenty-three years, until, in November, 1887, he was appointed to the Chair of Philosophy, rendered vacant by the death of his friend, E. M. Caro.

Paul Janet had taught in the École libre

des sciences politiques et sociales from the
time of its foundation in 1871, and his Lectures had grown in time into such books as
Saint-Simon et le Saint-Simonisme and *Les
origines du Socialisme contemporain*. In
1880, he became a member of the Conseil
Supérieur de l'Instruction Publique, as the
representative of the Faculty of Arts, and
he successfully defended the philosophical
studies, which, during the Eighties, were
being attacked, just as it is now the fashion,
in certain quarters, to denounce the systematic study of the classical languages. Janet
died on the 4th of October, 1899, shortly
after celebrating his golden wedding, sur-
rounded by his devoted wife, and thirteen
children and grandchildren.

As a philosopher, Paul Janet belongs to
the idealist school. It has been asserted by
some that he is not an original thinker, but
merely an echo of his great master Victor
Cousin. Nothing could be farther from the
truth. Proud of the title of disciple, he is,
indeed, a faithful follower of Cousin, and
through him of Hegel. He did undoubtedly
recognise that it was a part of his life work
to defend the old positions of Cousinist
spiritualism, which positive science and

economic speculation were challenging on every side. But he is much more than an imitator and continuator. Janet's true originality and real independence lie in the *method* by which he sought to conserve and establish upon sure foundations the essential doctrines of what Leibnitz calls *perennis philosophica*. Unlike many less profound thinkers of the Eclectic School, who, in the name of an easy-going common sense, had accepted a variety of heterogeneous philosophical propositions, incapable of logical and systematic co-ordination, Janet, while fully recognising the many-sided aspects of truth, sought to discover, and, I think, succeeded in setting forth luminously, the underlying unity of reason, and in satisfying all the legitimate aspirations of the soul.

His sympathetic and enlightened tolerance of all forms of honest search after truth was the outcome of his own open-mindedness and disinterested love of truth for its own sake. His liberalism always caused him to look for the soul of good in things evil, while his generosity led him to accept and welcome with gratitude the germ of truth in erroneous systems and decaying institutions. By this temper and method, he is akin to Maine de

INTRODUCTION

Biran, the father of the French Spiritualist School. Hence his impartial attitude towards a form of Christianity which was not his own, and, in particular, the attraction he felt for the person of Fénelon, a Prelate who, while he endeavoured to remain faithful to all that was best in the old forms of religious belief, and while he defended the traditions of classical antiquity, nevertheless held firmly to his vision of better things in the future, and is now ranked among the fearless pioneers, as a fellow-worker with the Spirit of Truth and Progress.

Janet's philosophy is essentially a dogmatic philosophy of conscience. Excellent, and often profound, as a dialectician, his method is in a high degree scientific. He discards all ethical systems based upon hedonistic or utilitarian considerations. His own position rests upon the recognition of a moral first cause, that is, upon a belief in the existence not merely of a transcendent God, but of an immanent Father, Who loves His creation, and Who, as Janet says, " en nous confiant le soin de faire arriver son règne, l'a rendu au moins possible en faisant le monde."

A voluminous philosophical writer, Janet

INTRODUCTION

will continue to be revered by the general reading public chiefly for his touching and inspiring book on *La Famille*, even as his master, Cousin, is remembered to-day principally for his stimulating work *Du Vrai, du Beau et du Bien*, published ten years earlier. But among professional philosophers, and serious students of thought, Janet will live as the author of *La Morale, les Causes Finales*, and especially *Principes de Métaphysique et de Psychologie*, which contains the most matured expression of his mind. This work, which he himself termed his " testament philosophique," obtained, in 1898, the Jean Reynaud Prize, the highest award of the Academy of Moral and Political Sciences, and one which is bestowed on the writer of the most remarkable work published during the preceding five years. In his masterly study of this important book, in an Article which appeared in the *Revue Philosophique* of November, 1897 (pp. 525–551), Henri Bergson wrote : " C'est le livre où M. Janet a mis le meilleur de sa pensée. . . . L'Œuvre philosophique de M. Janet est considérable. Répartie sur une période de près de cinquante années, elle a exercé une longue et profonde influence sur notre enseignement, et par là sur notre philosophie en général."

Paul Janet also wrote a large number of valuable pedagogical and political works and articles, in which he never loses sight of the close relationship between politics and ethics : he is rightly of opinion that all economic questions are at bottom moral questions. This may be seen in the very title of one of his greatest works, *Histoire de la science politique dans ses rapports avec la morale*, crowned both by the Academy of Moral and Political Sciences and by the French Academy, in which he carries his investigations into the philosophy of history up to the year 1788. In the *Philosophie de la Révolution Française*, he shows himself an enthusiastic admirer of that epoch-making document "La Déclaration des Droits de l'Homme et du Citoyen," while he often condemns the methods employed to bring about the triumph of principles essentially just and righteous.

No one was better qualified than Paul Janet to write an authoritative appreciation of his friend and master Victor Cousin, whose work he appraised in 1885. By no means a blind admirer, Janet has given us

INTRODUCTION

a monograph which is the best critical study we possess of the life-work and influence of the great educationist, historian, critic, and head of the Eclectic School.

Paul Janet is a literary critic of no mean order, but his best work is unfortunately scattered in the pages of such reviews as the *Journal des Savants*, and the *Revue des Deux Mondes;* it deals with a very wide range of subjects and with a great number of writers and thinkers of the last three centuries. Under the title of *Lectures variées de Littérature et de Morale*, Janet himself edited, in 1890, a volume of Extracts from his own works, a bold and unusual feat, and one which few philosophical writers could successfully perform. He also produced excellent translations, with introductions, of Saint Augustine's *Confessions*, and Spinoza's *Tractatulus de Deo et Homine ejusque Felicitate*.

A writer so catholic in his tastes and so universal in his activities, and one, moreover, who laboured unremittingly for half a century, was almost inevitably bound to make a personal and painstaking study of one of the most sympathetic and original figures of French theology and literature : the greatest character of the century of Louis

XIV, in so far as moral and spiritual qualities were concerned, Fénelon could not fail to appeal to a man of Janet's large-hearted tolerance, simplicity, and nobility of soul. Thus it is that, in the following pages, Janet gives us a conscientious and original study of Fénelon, and one which, owing to its straightforwardness and profound psychological insight, has been frequently quoted as authoritative by subsequent writers. But its chief merit is its clearness, that pre-eminently French intellectual quality, " héritage national," says Émile Boutroux, in his Notice on Paul Janet, " que nous avons le devoir de conserver et de transmettre à nos descendants."

Janet's name will long continue to carry weight as that of one of the worthiest representatives of spiritualistic philosophy during the XIXth century. One of the chief aides-de-camp of Cousin, he was both an original thinker and a theoretical writer, as well as a populariser of philosophical problems of practical interest, and especially of ethical questions, which constitute the favourite form of philosophising in France. He says in the Preface of one of his last works : " J'ai aimé la philosophie dans toutes ses parties, dans tous ses aspects, et dans toutes ses applications. Philosophie populaire, philosophie didactique, philosophie transcendante, morale, politique, application à la littérature et aux sciences, histoire de la philosophie, j'ai touché à tout, je me suis intéressé à tout : *nihil philosophicum a me alienum putavi.*"

His influence in France has been greater than that of any of the other disciples of Cousin, even Jules Simon and Caro. It has been a healthy influence, leading away from pure speculation to concrete results and activity of life. In his lectures, books, and articles, he ever laboured on behalf of the spiritualistic conception of the universe, and for an entente between philosophy and the various sciences. The enemy of all forms of pantheism, dogmatism, and pure empiricism, he attacked positivism and the materialistic metaphysics of Germany, and reacted against the contemporary anti-religious Schools of France, and against the tendency to make philosophy the hand-maiden of political parties, and in particular of the reactionary partisans of the Ancien Régime.

The dominant feature of Paul Janet's personality, and one which is reflected in his style, is dignified simplicity. This quality, which is also the most distinctive merit of Fénelon, as a man and a writer, is well defined in the following noble words of the Archbishop of Cambrai : " La simplicité est la droiture d'une âme qui s'interdit tout retour sur elle et sur ses actions. Cette vertu est différente de la sincérité, et la surpasse. On voit beaucoup de gens qui sont sincères sans être simples. Ils ne veulent passer que pour ce qu'ils sont, mais ils craignent sans cesse de passer pour ce qu'ils ne sont pas. L'homme simple n'affecte ni la vertu, ni la vérité même ; il n'est jamais occupé de lui, il semble avoir perdu ce moi dont on est si jaloux."

VICTOR LEULIETTE.

FÉNELON

HIS LIFE AND WORKS

CHAPTER I

YOUTH OF FÉNELON

" THIS Prelate was a tall, thin man, well-made, with a large nose, eyes whence fire and wit issued like a torrent, and a countenance such as I have never seen in any other person, and which, though seen but once, could never be forgotten. It combined everything, yet its contrasts did not conflict. It possessed gravity and courtesy, solemnity and gaiety ; it was equally expressive of the learned man, the Bishop, and the aristocrat : but what predominated in his face, as indeed in his whole person, was thought, intellect, grace, propriety, and above all nobility. One had to make an effort to cease looking at him."

So wrote Saint-Simon of the distinguished personage whose life-story we are about to relate, and of whose writings we shall here present an analysis. It can be said that

1

Fénelon's life and character, as well as his genius, agreed with the outward description of the man ; for here, too, everything was combined and in harmony, and the contrasts did not conflict. At once an ancient and a modern, a Christian and a man of the world, a mystic and a politician, unconventional and courtly, tractable and obstinate, simple and shrewd, attracting the Eighteenth century, as he had captivated the Seventeenth, as credulous as a child, and as bold as Spinoza, Fénelon is one of the most original figures which the Catholic Church has produced. We shall have to study in turn the various aspects of this rich nature. Let us begin with his family history.

François de Salignac de la Mothe-Fénelon was born at the Château de Fénelon, in Perigord, on the 6th of August, 1651. His family was an ancient one, and had distinguished itself in warfare and diplomacy. One of his great-great uncles, Bertrand Salignac de Fénelon, had been present at the siege of Metz with the Duke of Guise, and he has left us a manuscript diary of this siege. Later on, when Ambassador from the French Court to Queen Elizabeth, he was requested by the King to account for, and doubtless to justify, the massacre of Saint-Bartholomew. It is related that he replied with dignity : " Sire, question those who counselled it." Fénelon's father belonged to the younger branch of this family. He was twice married, and our author was born of the second marriage. He had brothers from the first marriage : the son of one of them, a nephew of Fénelon, known under the name of *Fanfan*, became as a son to him, after the loss of his father. In like manner, our Fénelon, having also lost his father at an early age, had become as a son to his uncle, the Marquis of Fénelon, who looked after his education.

He spent his early boyhood, until the age of twelve, in his father's Château, on account of his delicate health. Little is told us about his first education, save that it was Christian ; but we may well imagine that it was also enriched with classical literature and a knowledge of antiquity. When twelve years old, he was sent to the University of Cahors, where he finished his study of the humanities and philosophy.

We are not told the date at which Fénelon lost his father, but we know that from the time of his arrival in Paris he was under the guardianship of his uncle, the Marquis of Fénelon, a nobleman full of honour and piety, who, after losing his son at the siege of Candia, bestowed on his nephew the affection which had hitherto centred upon this son. The Marquis of Fénelon was intimately connected with the founder of the Community of Saint-Sulpice, Abbé Olier, who was his spiritual director. It was on his advice that he had his nephew admitted into the Seminary of Saint-Sulpice. We could wish for more details than Fénelon's biographers have left us concerning the beginnings of his vocation for the Church. The first motions of so noble a soul and so brilliant an imagination would possess a charm and an interest of which we are per-force deprived. Were there not signs in Fénelon's youth of that element of mundanity, worldliness, and well-nigh of pagan-ism, which was allied to the strongest religious devotion ? Were not his relatives disquieted by his graces which were so eminently refined and attractive ? Did he ask of his own accord to purify himself by religion, renouncement, and self-surrender to God ? Or was he merely placed there because family pride settled on his person the highest

worldly hopes in the ecclesiastical calling ?
We know nothing about this ; but what we
do know is that not the shadow of a regret,
a doubt, or a look backward, can be detected
in any of the writings, thoughts, and emotions
of the future Archbishop of Cambrai. Happy
times when it was possible to be so clever,
to depict so vividly the ardent love of
Eucharis, to converse so exquisitely on the
education of girls, to take so keen a pleasure
in the beauties of pagan art, to take part
in political life, and to obtain the highest
favours of the Court, without any of these
things proving detrimental to faith, the love
of God, or the highest form of mysticism !
Everything seems to induce us to believe
that it was a true vocation, an inborn piety,
that led Fénelon to the foot of the altar.
So he became a priest, and although he may
have a singular fascination for us because
of the peculiar mixture of nature and grace
in him, no one has a right to say that it is
at the expense of his Christian authority
and religious sincerity.

Fénelon, therefore, entered Saint-Sulpice
and pursued all his theological studies there
under the superintendence of Abbé Tronson,
in whom he always reposed the utmost

confidence, and for whom he ever entertained the deepest devotion. He took Holy Orders at about the age of twenty-four. He had had time to mature this decision ; and it may be said that such an age is a guarantee of the sincerity and earnestness which he exhibited in this matter. Nevertheless, the romantic turn of imagination which characterises Fénelon could not but display itself during his youth ; and it was manifested at this time, not indeed by tastes inconsistent with his holy vocation, but by a kind of ardent zeal which made him hanker after the most adventurous enterprises. Thus we see him for a time filled with enthusiasm about a mission in Asia Minor and the Levant, and especially in Greece, whither he dreams of going in order to catechise the hapless Christian victims of Turkish barbarism and tyranny. Sacred and profane recollections throng together as he writes, and in a letter (15th of October, 1675) to an unknown correspondent, he lets himself go with all the generous ardour of youth. " I am starting, my lord, I might almost say I am flying ; but I am contemplating a greater journey. The whole of Greece opens out before me, the Sultan retreats in dismay ; the Peloponnesus breathes freely again, and the Church of Corinth is about to flourish anew. . . . I am seeking that Areopagus where Saint Paul declared the unknown God to the wise men of this world ; but after the sacred comes the secular, and I shall not disdain to go down to the Piraeus, where Socrates outlined the plan of his Republic. I shall ascend the double summit of Parnassus ; I shall cull the laurels of Delphi, and taste the delights of Tempe. I shall not forget thee, O island hallowed by the heavenly visions of the beloved disciple, O blessed Patmos ! I shall go and kiss the footsteps of the Apostle, and shall fancy I see the heavens open before me ! " [1]

We cannot fail to recognise in this beautiful letter, and in these missionary aspirations, a kind of exuberance of youthful life and zeal, which the regular duties of the clerical profession failed to satisfy completely. Likewise, does not this curious blending of a twin enthusiasm, both for sacred and profane things, already reveal in his rich and refined nature that element of romance and poetry, which we shall recognise later in his writings.

[1] *Correspondance de Fénelon*, ii, p. 290.

One would also like to think, with Cardinal de Bausset, that it was similarly our Fénelon who, in his youthful days, filled with a divine passion for martyrdom, had boldly resolved to devote himself to mission work in Canada. One of Abbé Tronson's letters to Fénelon's uncle, the Bishop of Sarlat, acquaints us with this resolve which the Bishop deprecated. But the editors of the correspondence would seem to have proved that the letter of Abbé Tronson concerning this affair referred not to Fénelon himself, who at the date of this letter was only fifteen and a half, but to his eldest brother, a Sulpician like himself, who did in fact leave for Canada in 1667 (at the time the letter was written), and who died there in 1679. It cannot therefore relate to our Fénelon ; but the event itself shows that there existed in the family a romantic and adventurous turn of imagination, and that it combined religious fervour with poetry.

Meanwhile the time had come to pass from dreams to actions. Fénelon had completed his theological studies. He was a priest, and had just left Saint-Sulpice. A post suited to his passionate inclination towards propaganda and proselytism was sought for him. It was neither in Canada, like his brother, nor in the East, but in Paris itself that Fénelon was called upon to serve the Christian cause by displaying his missionary zeal. The Archbishop of Paris appointed him Superior of a recently formed Community, *Les Nouvelles Catholiques*. These were young women, recently converted from Protestantism, who required to be continued and maintained in the faith. Nothing was more agreeable to the tastes, and, if in such a matter we may be allowed so secular an expression, to the talent of Fénelon. It is well known how greatly he distinguished himself at a later period as a spiritual director, so much so that he even attracted the soul, so cold and hard, at least to all appearances, of Mme. de Maintenon. Gentleness, grace, good sense, elegant and ornate fluency of speech, all these qualities of a father confessor, he possessed in the highest degree. Doubtless he exercised them with power and success in the little Community of which he was the Head, for he was soon entrusted with a task far more laborious and difficult, namely, the work of a missioner in France among the inhabitants

FÉNELON

of Saintonge and Poitou, recently reclaimed from the Protestant faith, or yet to be converted. Thus Fénelon found himself connected with the important events of the Revocation of the Edict of Nantes.[1] What was his own conviction in the matter? What was his conduct throughout? What was the real trend of his thought in this all-important crisis? This is one of the most complex and momentous points we have to elucidate.

For a long time there prevailed a bias on this question, which the most recent criticism has definitely dispelled, although this bias was not in every point erroneous. We know that the eighteenth century bestowed upon Fénelon a reputation for a species of tolerantism and philosophy in agreement with the ideas then in vogue under the influence of Voltaire.[2] Chénier devoted a tragedy to Fénelon which had its hour of success during the Revolutionary period (February, 1793).[3] The author put the following philosophical lines into the mouth of the hero:

[1] *Cf.* Note i, p. 257.
[2] *Cf.* Note ii, p. 258.
[3] *Cf.* Note iii, p. 259.

10

L'erreur n'est pas un crime aux yeux de l'Éternel ;
N'exigez donc pas plus que n'exige le ciel :
Sous nos cinq derniers rois, la seule intolérance
A fait un siècle entier les malheurs de la France. . . .
La douceur et le temps combleront nos désirs ;
Et jamais la rigueur n'a fait que des martyrs.

La Harpe,[1] in his *Éloge de Fénelon,* which was crowned by the French Academy, likewise extolled Fénelon's tolerance. On the other hand, Abbé de Boulogne [2] published during the Restoration a memoir on *la Prétendue Tolérance de Fénelon,* in which he exonerated him from this supposed virtue which the philosophers had imputed to him. In our day, a learned writer, Orentin Douen,[3] has protested most strongly against what he terms *la légende de Fénelon.* Eugène Despois,[4] a champion of Fénelon, contented himself with pleading extenuating circumstances. Finally, the publication in their entirety of the letters from Saintonge, addressed to Seignelay, only two or three of which figured in the great edition of 1827,[5] has provided all the documents necessary for a full examination of the case. What is the outcome of all this critical labour ? [6]

[1] *Cf.* Note iv, p. 260.   [4] *Cf.* Note vii, p. 260.
[2] *Cf.* Note v, p. 260.   [5] *Cf.* Note viii, p. 260.
[3] *Cf.* Note vi, p. 260.   [6] *Cf.Correspondance,* i,p. 3.

FÉNELON

We have then Fénelon's letters, in which he gives an account of his mission in Poitou, addressed to M. de Seignelay, and also one to Bossuet [1] on the same subject. In no passage of these letters, and in none of his other writings, do we come across so much as the shadow of a complaint against the act of the Revocation. Doubtless such an expression of disapprobation would have been somewhat ill-timed, Fénelon himself being in a measure entrusted with the execution of the King's orders. He was young, and in all the fervour of religious faith. It was scarcely the time to think of philosophy. He never made the slightest request that authority should cease to make its sway felt over the new converts; on the contrary, he says that "it is important that those who are in authority should support him." He even ordered that care should be exercised to "combine vigilance in the matter of desertions, and *rigorous penalties* against recusants, with all the resources of Christian persuasion." He denounced to the Secretary of State the evasive methods of the unfortunate Huguenots who wanted to fly abroad, and recommended an increase

[1] *Cf. Correspondance de Fénelon*, ii, p. 196.

in the number of guards between Bordeaux and the coast. He demanded the strict punishment of renegades. He complained of the newly converted officers who were slack in the performance of their duties. He called for the banishment of a few of the leaders to Canada. It seems as though he even approved of drawing on a hurdle the corpses of those who had refused the sacraments.[1] It is therefore very difficult to maintain that Fénelon was not a believer in the right of the government to make use of force against heretics, and even that he did not for his part co-operate in the employment of such means.

Nevertheless, what cannot be denied is the fact of his having given the preference to gentle and persuasive methods rather than to violent measures. In the very letters we have just quoted, Fénelon expressly counsels kindness and patience. "It would be easy for us," he writes, "to force them to go to confession and take communion, if we were willing to press them in order to advance the reputation of our missions. But would it not be a vain pretence to bring to confession those who do

[1] *Cf.* Note ix, p. 261.

not yet acknowledge the true Church, and
her power to remit sins ? How shall we
give Jesus Christ to those who do not believe
they receive Him ? Yet I am aware that
in those places where the missionaries and
the troops are side by side, the new converts go together to communion. And yet
these people, hard, obstinate, and embittered
against our religion, are cowardly and self-
interested. If you press them only a little,
you will see them perpetrate countless acts
of sacrilege ; you will only provoke them
to despair by the remorse of their conscience,
or else you will throw them into a state of
callousness and religious indifference, which
is the height of impiety. In so far as we
are concerned, we should expect to draw
down upon our heads a horrible curse, if
we rested content with hastily performing
a merely superficial piece of work, which
might wear a dazzling appearance from a
distance." These sentiments are obviously
full of charity and benignity, and in an eminent degree Christian. We see, in reality, two
systems in presence : on one side, an ad-
ministrative and political system, which considered and desired only outward submission,
and cared little for the inner consciousness.

14

The aim was to be able to inform the King that there were no more Huguenots, even if the latter had been replaced by atheists. The great concern was not about the soul, but about a purely political obedience. Those who carried too far the system of kindness, were reproached for their excessive forbearance and patience : this was the attitude taken up by Fénelon, although he never denied or doubted the rights of civil authority ; but he was Christian enough to perceive that the system was powerless to secure truly religious results. He had himself won his way into the confidence of the new converts by the charm and grace of his methods. He expressed the wish "that these good beginnings might be strengthened by discreet preachers who should combine skill in instruction with the art of gaining the confidence of the people." Furthermore, he desired "the new Intendant not to exercise an uncompromising authority which would render him odious." While not denying the rights of authority which, he admitted, ought to be unrelenting in its efforts to keep the Huguenots within the kingdom, he nevertheless added that "it is a matter of importance that they should find in France sufficient allurements to deprive them of any inclination to quit the country." However exaggerated the opinion of the eighteenth century may have been concerning Fénelon's tolerantism, we see that it was not wholly a legend, and that he must have left a certain memory, a kind of tradition of moderation and benevolence, for the reputation which attaches to his name to have become established. In default of a philosophical impartiality, which nothing warranted in Fénelon's time, it was no mean achievement to have set, under such sorry circumstances, an example of kindliness and humanity.

Let us complete the picture of this first period, which corresponds with Fénelon's youth, by the account he gives his cousin, the Marchioness of Laval, of his entry into Carennac, a benefice which had been bestowed upon him by his uncle, the Bishop of Sarlat. It will be seen that Fénelon was open no less to the blitheness of youth, than to its enthusiasm and generous ardour. Might we not imagine we were reading a letter inspired by Mme. de Sévigné in the following narrative ? " I advanced escorted in majestic style by all the delegates, and

I noticed that the entire population was lining the quay in crowds. Two boats filled with the elite of the townspeople drew near, and I perceived that, by a courteous stratagem, the best disciplined troops of the district had concealed themselves in a corner of the beautiful island which you know; in fine battle array they proceeded to salute me with repeated volleys of musketry; the air was already quite darkened with the smoke of so many discharges, and nothing was now heard but the dreadful reports of gunpowder. The fiery steed on which I was mounted, filled with a noble ardour, tried to plunge into the water; but I was more restrained, so I dismounted. . . . I then reached the gate, the consuls began their harangue; you may well imagine the spirit and pomp of their encomium. The orator compared me to the sun; soon after I was the moon; after that all the other radiant luminaries had the honour of being likened to me, and we ended up felicitously with the beginning of the world! By that time the sun had retired, so I went to my bedchamber and prepared to do likewise." [1] We see that

[1] *Cf. Correspondance*, ii, p. 9. Letter of May 22, 1681.

FÉNELON

Fénelon, in spite of his sensibility and the nobility of his soul, did not disdain to laugh, and that he was also able to detect the ridiculous aspects of the people he met. It is regrettable that this amiable and humorous note should be so rare in his writings. This letter and the following one (June 16), concerning a legal case, ludicrously conducted at Carennac by the Ciceros of the place, constitute the only evidence we possess of his youthful liveliness. Graver preoccupations were soon to fill his life.

CHAPTER II

" DE L'ÉDUCATION DES FILLES "

THE first work published by Fénelon was the treatise *De l'Éducation des Filles*, which appeared in 1687.[1] In the mind of the author, this was at first nothing more than a private composition, written at the request of the Duke and Duchess of Beauvillier, Fénelon's great friends, who desired to be guided by his advice in the education of their children, and especially of their daughters. This writing seemed to them so rich in solid and discriminating thoughts, and so suitable for the instruction of persons of all ranks, that they persuaded Fénelon to publish it.

Fénelon's treatise is the real starting-point of French pedagogy on this important question. Before it, there was nothing. " It will doubtless be a great paradox," said Abbé Fleury, a friend of Fénelon, " to maintain that women ought to know anything beyond their catechism, sewing, and sundry kinds of fancy work, singing, dancing, how to bow gracefully and speak correctly ; for

[1] *Cf.* Note x, p. 261.

their education usually consists in these things alone." As often happens, such an extremity of ignorance led rather more independent minds into the opposite paradox. In 1672, fourteen years before Fénelon, Poulain de la Barre, a Protestant writer, had published his treatise *De l'Égalité des Sexes*, in which he said: "If it were considered ridiculous to see a woman teaching oratory and medicine, engaging in police work, delivering a harangue before judges as a barrister, administering justice, leading an army, etc., it would only be because the sight were a novel one; people would get used to it." We see then that the boldest ideas of our day, and those furthest removed from actual practice, had crossed the mind of a philosopher of the seventeenth century; yet, in reality, far from advancing towards this equality, the instruction of women was absolutely and systematically neglected; people appeared to accept in daily life the maxim of the unsophisticated Chrysale, who deemed it enough for a woman

Quand la capacité de son esprit se hausse
A connaître un pourpoint d'avec un haut-de-chausse. [1]

[1] *Cf.* Note xi, p. 261.

"DE L'ÉDUCATION DES FILLES"

So much may be inferred from Fénelon's opening words :

"Nothing is more neglected than the education of girls. . . . They must not be learned, people say ; curiosity makes them vain and affected ; it is enough if they know how to manage their prospective households, and obey their husbands without arguing. People do not fail to turn to account the experience they have of many women whom knowledge has rendered ridiculous : upon which they imagine they have a right to surrender daughters blindly to the guidance of ignorant and imprudent mothers."

Yet Fénelon is certainly far from desirous of turning women into blue-stockings ; and he seems to be replying indirectly to Poulain de la Barre, when he says that " they ought neither to govern the State (a thing which they have nevertheless done in more than one instance, and with success), nor wage war, nor enter the sacred ministry." But while thus reiterating in an ironical form the objections of the adversaries of women's education, who, of course, considered as usual only its excesses, Fénelon did not allow himself to be shaken by these objections.

He would not have women limit their minds to the management of their households and to obedience to their husbands. He shows, on the contrary, the great function of woman in the home and in the State. People plead the weakness of their sex ; but " the weaker they are, the more they require to be strengthened. . . . Have they not duties to perform ? They it is who ruin or uphold the home, and who have the principal share in good or bad morals. . . . Even the concerns of the outer world are not foreign to them, because of the influence they exercise over their husbands and children. . . . Can men hope for any amenities in their own lives if their most intimate relationship, marriage itself, turns into vexation ? What will become of the children, who will in due time constitute the whole of the human race, if the mothers spoil them from their very first years ? " The conclusion is obvious : if boys are brought up with so much care, because of the important tasks they will have to perform in the world, how can we neglect the education of women, who are entrusted with the early education of boys ?

The governing principle of Fénelon's book

is that of the dignity of woman, whence the necessity of instructing her and of improving her mind. Nothing more liberal than this conception could have been devised, nor anything more in conformity with the claims of the future.

Indeed, if one thing more than another is characteristic of Fénelon's work, it is this anticipation of the future, and this spirit of liberty which causes us to recognise ourselves, and to discover the germs of our modern ideas, in this charming little book. To be sure, we must not consider any specific prescription, nor search in his programme for any particular subject-matter of education. This programme of his would perhaps appear somewhat modest and rather curtailed in comparison with our own to-day, but what interests us even more than his conclusions, is the spirit that inspires them ; for this spirit is in a high degree liberal. Fénelon, long before Rousseau, claimed that we should learn from nature,[1] that we should not inflict upon children a material training, deadening to their activities and revolting to their age. He felt the charm of childhood, and loved children. That is why he

[1] *Cf.* Note xii, p. 262.

is a great educationist, and one of the masters of French pedagogy.

Let us return to the need for instructing girls : " The ignorance of a girl," says Fénelon, " is the reason why she feels dull and does not know how to busy herself innocently." If her mind be not applied from childhood to solid matters, " all serious things seem dreary to her ; anything which requires sustained attention wearies her ; propensity for pleasure, the example of persons of the same age, everything makes her fear a regular and industrious life. . . . Lack of application becomes an incurable habit."

Ignorance is no preservative against frivolity. Idleness, on the contrary, produces " a pernicious inclination for entertainments and dramatic performances." Persons who are well-instructed, and accustomed to serious matters, have no curiosity for useless subjects. But ignorance, or inferior instruction, leads to " a wandering imagination which turns towards vain and dangerous objects."

Fénelon does not seem to follow his own line of thought when he asserts that these badly brought up girls, if they are intelligent, become either blue-stockings, who discourse on wit and live on romantic adventures, or else controversialists, who decide about religious problems, as the fashion often was in the seventeenth century. These defects would appear to belong to learned, rather than to ignorant women.[1] Yet there is no inconsistency in the mind of Fénelon. Doubtless, even when badly trained, an intelligent girl will naturally turn towards intellectual pursuits, which she will carry to too great lengths ; she will thus become a blue-stocking, a theologian, or a free-thinker, without a sound knowledge of anything, and in all matters adopting false views. Ignorance does not offer a guarantee against these abuses, rather it favours them, because it furnishes no aim or counterpoise to the wandering imagination. On the other hand, a well-trained and cultivated mind will know how to fortify itself against the absurdities of false science and erroneous theology.

Besides, these are only the mistakes of intellectual persons ; the rest, endowed with no less curiosity, but not aiming so high, will betake themselves to the things proportioned to their mentality : " to know

[1] *Cf.* Note xiii, p. 262.

what is being said and done, a song, a piece of news, an intrigue; to receive letters, and read those of other people. They are vain, and vanity makes them talk a great deal; they are frivolous, and frivolity inhibits those considerations which would often cause them to remain silent."

Fénelon lays down the true principle of a liberal education, when he says: "As far as possible, girls are to be led by reason." To many minds, this is a principle of disorder and anarchy. According to them, it is not to reason, but to authority, that we are to resort. The child must obey, whether he does or does not know the reason why. If he understands the reason, it is no longer you, but himself that he is obeying, and that is not obedience. You are teaching him to be his own master, and thereby to emancipate himself from authority. Modern anarchy is therefore wholly summed up in these words: to be led by reason. But these are precisely the consequences which make us say that Fénelon's book is inspired by a quite modern spirit, and by a point of view which unconsciously glimpses the future. For it is the master endeavour of modern education to see to it that each one, according to the measure of his power, shall become his own master, obeying no external orders, but his own reason alone, that is to say, himself. To-day, society as a whole is advancing in this direction, and for this purpose it is not sufficient to subject children to a material rule from without, they must be made to understand the wherefore of their actions. Does that mean that children are to be addressed as men ? No, unquestionably ; for we are dealing with the reason of a child, and not with reason in general ; we have to adapt our advice to the comprehension of his small intelligence, and to deem this impossible is not to know children. They readily understand, on the contrary, the reasons which are given them, and one is sometimes surprised to perceive the ease with which they grasp what is told them. Does it then follow that this method may always be employed ? Certainly not, and Fénelon is careful to say : " As far as possible." We know that angry children no longer hear nor understand ; so, when necessary, we cannot forego the use of force, I do not say in order to strike them, but to compel them : for example, to remove from their hands the dangerous implement which might cut them, or to take them up bodily in order to put them to bed ; no education will ever be able to dispense with these summary means. But what is useless and oppressive, is authority in season and out of season ; that violent, imperious, scolding tone adopted by common women towards their children, which ends by losing all efficacy when it is never-ceasing ; and, above all, it is the theory that you must crush the will of the child : a will that has been crushed is no longer of any service, the child remaining as open to evil as to good influences. Instead of destroying the will, you must develop it, and this can only be done by uniting it with its natural guide, reason.

Another point of originality in Fénelon, and one which makes him sometimes speak like Montaigne,[1] is the fact that he associates the idea of pleasure with that of virtue. Perhaps Saint-Cyran, perhaps Bossuet himself, would have been severe towards this over-agreeable type of education ; but Fénelon does not go beyond the bounds of moderation, and he seems to us to be in the right when he says : " Mingle teaching and play ; let wisdom show herself to the child

[1] *Cf.* Note xiv, p. 262.

only at intervals, and with a smiling face. If he forms a sad and gloomy conception of virtue, all is lost."

What could be more amiable and tender, and withal more sensible, than the following advice : " Never, save in cases of absolute necessity, assume an austere and imperious air which makes children tremble, for they are usually only too timid and bashful. You would harden their hearts and destroy that confidence without which no benefits are to be expected from education. Make yourself loved by them ; let them be free with you and not afraid to let you see all their faults."

This condescension towards children is not the foe of authority : "If the wise man has bidden us hold the rod constantly raised over the child, if he has said that a father who plays with his own son will live to weep, it is not because he disapproved of a kindly and patient education. He is only con-demning those thoughtless parents who gratify the passions of their children, and seek merely to amuse them." Moreover, Fénelon does not deny that there are children who can only be mastered by fear ; this is then an expedient which it is permissible to employ, albeit only when it is impossible to do otherwise.

So charming a pedagogue, and one so kindly disposed towards the child, will not be in favour of what is known to-day as *surmenage*.[1] More must not be required of children than their tender and sensitive age can give : " One frequently demands of children a degree of punctuality and seriousness, of which those who exact it would themselves be incapable. No freedom, no merriness, but always lessons, silence, uncomfortable postures, reprimands, and threats." Fénelon, who was an Ancient in so far as imagination was concerned, appeals on this point to the example of the Ancients : " It was by means of poetry and music that the principal sciences, the maxims of virtue, and the refinement of manners, were introduced among the Hebrews, the Egyptians, and the Greeks." What he fears above all else is the effects of fear and terror : " Joy and confidence should be their ordinary condition ; otherwise their minds are obscured, and their spirits broken ; if they be quick, they are provoked to anger ; if they be indolent, they are stupefied. Fear

[1] *Cf.* Note xv, p. 263.

"DE L'ÉDUCATION DES FILLES"

is like those violent remedies which are used in cases of extreme illness : they purge, but they impair the constitution and destroy the organs ; a soul dominated by fear is always weakened thereby."

Other counsels also forestall the most modern ideas. Fénelon preconises what we call to-day object lessons.[1] The following is an excellent summary of this method of teaching :

"In the country, they see a windmill and they want to know what it is : you must show them how the food that nourishes man is prepared. Further on they descry reapers : you must explain to them what they are doing, how the corn is sown, and how it grows in the earth. In the town they see shops, in which various crafts are practised and divers wares sold : you will then teach them by degrees the process of manufacture of all the articles which are used by man, and which commerce deals with. Little by little, and without special studies, they will learn the right way to make these things, and the exact value of each. This kind of knowledge is particularly interesting to girls."

[1] *Cf.* Note xvi, p. 263.

FÉNELON

In Fénelon's time, and according to his own testimony, an extremely ridiculous way of teaching children how to read prevailed. They were made to read Latin in a declamatory tone. Such a method was bound to disgust children, and how protracted it must also have been, in view of its difficulty and tediousness! Fénelon, on the contrary, advises the use of story books, where children will learn to read by themselves and with the greatest facility. He does not disdain to appeal to their eyes, as we also appeal to-day : " You must give them. well-bound books, with gilt edges even, and with beautiful pictures." Likewise, in teaching them writing, he will set children to write about objects which are familiar to them and which personally interest them. " Write me a note, one might say ; inform your brother or your cousin of such and such an occurrence : all that will please the child, provided no dull picture of a set lesson disturbs him." In a word, Fénelon complains that under ordinary educational systems, " all the delight is located on the one side, and all the boredom on the other." He was also acquainted with the principle of *short sessions*, of which a utopist of our day,

"DE L'ÉDUCATION DES FILLES"

Charles Fourier, imagined himself to be the discoverer : " Let their attention wander a little ; allow them even from time to time to indulge in some recreation or games, in order that their minds may roam about freely ; then bring them back by degrees to the end in view."

Although he is the enemy of all extremes, it is nevertheless evident that Fénelon prefers vitality and warmth of blood to overmuch passivity in a child. The hardest thing in education appears to him to be the task of influencing children " who are deficient in sensibility." Although he was not yet at this time Tutor to the Duke of Burgundy, he seems by anticipation to contrast the character of this Prince with that of the Dauphin, the pupil of Bossuet : " Lively and sensitive characters are prone to terrible excesses ; but they have great resources and often return from afar. . . . One has the wherewithal to interest them in what they are being taught, and to appeal to their sense of honour, but one has no hold over indolent natures. Not that we are to rely too much on an active and amiable disposition ; one is often greatly deceived in this way, because the early graces of a child are a lustre which conceals all else. We see in them something indescribably moving and winsome, which forbids our examining closely and in detail the features of the countenance. At every evidence of intelligence in them we stand amazed ; even their errors of judgment possess the charm of ingenuousness."—"But these are only outward appearances. Such an one who, at the age of five, was remarkable for his cleverness, has since fallen into obscurity and contempt. One thing only we can build upon, and that is good reasoning powers."

All this general advice is equally applicable to every form of education and to all children. Let us consider more closely that part which concerns girls. Here Fénelon reveals himself as a refined psychologist, and he shows us that the faults of girls are no less known to him than those of boys. He is of opinion that the education of girls, as it was given in his day, was too unprogressive and spiritless. You must render girls capable of firm and orderly conduct. It is only affectation that accustoms them to make a show of imaginary fears and to weep for nothing. You must repress petty jealousies, extravagant compliments, flattery, and everything that spoils them and indisposes them towards what they consider dry and austere. They are very artful and expert in the use of long roundabout means in order to attain their ends : "They have a natural facility for playing all sorts of parts ; tears cost them nothing ; their passions are strong, and their knowledge is limited." Moreover, they are timid, and therefore all the more given to dissimulate : "Point out to them how one can be discreet and guarded, without being deceitful ; add further that what cunning devises is mean and despicable, . . . and that it always proceeds from an ignoble heart and a small mind." Above all, be careful not to commend them when they have shown some adroitness by an act of duplicity : "By praising them for such faults, you persuade them that it is clever to be sly."

From the wiliness and make-believe of girls, Fénelon passes on to consider the coquettishness which usually accompanies these defects. "Girls are born," he says, "with a violent desire to please ; they are passionately fond of adornments ; a head-dress, a bit of ribbon, a curl placed higher or lower, the choice of a colour, all these

things are serious matters in their eyes."
He observes that this failing is peculiarly
characteristic of the French nation,[1] which
combines "a love of finery with a passion
for novelty : these two manias destroy the
boundaries between the classes, and entirely
corrupt manners." The origin of all this
mischief lies in the power wielded by women.
"Teach girls that the honour which comes
from good conduct is more to be prized than
that which is derived from their hair and
their garments." By an excess of austerity,
which seems out of harmony with the
general spirit of the work, he even goes so far
as to deprecate beauty, which, he says, is of
little other use than "to cause a girl to make
a profitable marriage." That is not such
a small matter after all ; and such a pros-
pect is not greatly calculated to give a distaste for it either to girls or their parents.
But he adds that beauty will not attain this
end unless it be enhanced by merit and
virtue. Otherwise, beauty by itself will con-
sign her to some madcap or other who will
make her unhappy. Careful attention to
one's beauty soon makes one ridiculous
when such care outlasts youth.

[1] *Cf.* Note xvii, p. 264.

"DE L'ÉDUCATION DES FILLES"

After beauty comes apparel, and Fénelon does not think it beneath his dignity to offer advice on this frivolous subject : frivolous only in appearance, for how great a part apparel plays in the history both of womankind and of morals! Fénelon does not affect an air of gloomy austerity ; he does not enjoin upon women of the world the indifference of nuns for bodily adornments ; rather he speaks as an artist and a man of taste : " I would have young girls see," he says, " the noble simplicity which is visible in the statues and other figures, which have come down to us, of Greek and Roman women ; they would then perceive how graceful and majestic it is to wear the hair carelessly plaited at the back, and full and flowing drapery with long folds. It were well if they had an enlightened appreciation for painters and all who have a keen discernment of antiquity." Thus Fénelon is disposed to impart to girls a taste for, and a superficial knowledge of, the fine arts, if only in order to influence their toilet, and to bring a feeling for what is noble and refined to bear upon it ; not, of course, that he counsels young girls to dress in Grecian style, as was done under the Directoire ;

but they would thus acquire a liking for " that dignified simplicity which is so consonant with the Christian way of life." Moreover, like all Christian pastors, he inveighs against all forms of immodesty in attire, pointing out, with uncompromising boldness, that women are accomplices in the passions which they excite : " When they strive to please, what is their aim ? To excite the passions of men. What weapons do they hold in their hands to restrain them ? If men go too far, must not women charge themselves with all the consequences ? You are preparing a subtle and mortal poison, and you think yourselves innocent ? "

Consider now the conclusions at which Fénelon arrives. It is here that he seems to us rather narrow, after having appeared almost too liberal. He seems to confine this instruction to a knowledge of how to speak and write correctly, and to familiarity with the four rules of arithmetic. He would also give them some acquaintance with law, that they should know, for example, the difference between a will and a donation, the nature of a contract, an entail, a deed of division, personal and real estate ; but he warns them against chicanery, to which women are greatly inclined. Finally, he gives a place, albeit a limited one, to the culture of the mind, to " the reading of such profane books as present no dangers for the passions, more particularly Greek and Roman history, and even the history of France, which has also its elements of beauty." Thus French history is scarcely more than a concession, instead of being, as it should be, a fundamental branch of study. He disapproves of the learning of Italian and Spanish, " which only serve to read books that are pernicious and calculated to aggravate the faults of women." Furthermore, he sanctions, but with nice discrimination, the reading of works of eloquence and poetry, if due care be taken not to set on fire their over-strong imaginations. " The more everything suggestive of the passion of love is softened down and half-concealed, the more dangerous it appears to me." The same applies to painting and music, which Fénelon admits, but with the same safeguards. Even so, he would have us limit ourselves to Christian and religious music. Painting is less perilous.

On the whole, this syllabus of studies may perhaps appear somewhat timorous to us in these days : in particular, that part of it which concerns the culture and adornment of the mind is too sparingly encouraged ; but, for Fénelon's time, it must be regarded as at once broad and daring : all those half sanctions, which seem to us to proceed from over-caution, were bold innovations. He it was who gave the impulse towards a broader scope in feminine education. Moreover—and this is a fact which has nothing to do with the question of his educational programme—no work ever treated better of women, with more taste, delicacy, and insight ; a style full of ease and charm, as refined as it is lucid, " albeit slightly dragging," is the one best suited to the subject.

Fénelon had laid down the principles of a sound education. He was shortly to be called upon to put them to the test.

CHAPTER III

FÉNELON AS TUTOR TO THE DUKE OF BURGUNDY

THE year 1689 is all-important in Fénelon's career. He was then thirty-eight years of age. Relinquishing the humble functions of Convent Chaplain, he now made his appearance at Court in the capacity of Tutor to a Prince. This was the time when the Court, after the example of Louis XIV, was beginning to amend its ways. Having grown wise with age, this monarch had renounced his unbridled amours in favour of more regular bonds. He had substituted a friend for a mistress, Mme. de Maintenon for Mme. de Montespan ; and the Queen's death had supervened in time to furnish the new favourite with an opportunity for a lawful union. The new Tutor soon became one of Mme. de Maintenon's intimate friends, and for a while it seemed as though Fénelon were on the road to fortune and power.

At this critical time in Fénelon's career, it is fitting to recall the confused and deceptive judgment which Saint-Simon has expressed on him. He had a fairly close acquaintance with Fénelon, being of his circle ; and, were it not for the known malevolence of his peevish nature, one would be inclined to imagine that no one was in a better position to give us an insight into the true character and mental outlook of our hero.

" Fénelon," Saint-Simon tells us, " was a man of capacity who had nothing, and who, conscious of much intellect, and of that kind of insinuating and fascinating intellect which accompanies many talents and graces, and much knowledge, was also very ambitious. He had long been knocking at every door, without having succeeded in gaining admittance anywhere. Incensed against the Jesuits, and vexed at being unable to find favour with them, he turned to the Jansenists to console himself, and succeeded in being invited to their private repasts. . . . I know not whether he appeared to them too shrewd, but little by little his connection with them cooled, and by dint of hovering around Saint-Sulpice, he succeeded in forming another, from which he expected better things." [1]

[1] *Cf.* Saint-Simon, *Mémoires,* i, p. 284 (Chéruel's edition).

FÉNELON AS TUTOR

It is not easy to verify Saint-Simon's assertions on the subject of Fénelon's relations with the Jesuits and Jansenists in the early part of his career ; no one, however, can fail to marvel that a mind of such quality and charm could have been successively spurned by these so powerful associations, which must have been eager to gain recruits at all costs ; and, of course, the chance of obtaining such a recruit did not occur every day. But, besides the small likelihood of a double repulse, it is easy for us to rectify Saint-Simon's statements concerning Fénelon's relations with the Sulpicians. It is not accurate to say that " by dint of hovering around Saint-Sulpice, he succeeded in forming a connection." Indeed we know that such was not the case. It was immediately on the termination of his humanities that his uncle placed him in the Seminary of Saint-Sulpice to pursue his theological studies. He had therefore not had time to carry on intrigues in connection with the Jesuits and the Jansenists. Having been trained at Saint-Sulpice, he entered, in the most natural manner possible, into close intimacy with his teachers. Abbé Tronson, his spiritual director, was one of the masters of the Community. Fénelon's relations with Saint-Sulpice were, therefore, those of a scholar with his old school. It may well have happened, of course, that Fénelon, who had an overwhelming desire to please, and " whose conceited mind aimed at being appreciated, even by workmen and valets," may, in the irresponsible days of his youth, have had relations with the Jesuits and the Jansenists ; but his intimacy with Saint-Sulpice is of earlier date, and did not originate in his alleged rebuff in another quarter.

Let us now consider what Saint-Sulpice was at this time, according to Saint-Simon : " This Society was just beginning to make its way. Ignorance, the pettiness of its practices, lack of protection, and the want of members of distinction in any way, inspired the company with a blind obedience to Rome. This seemed a convenient middle-way to prelates." If we make some deductions on account of the habitually captious tone which pervades Saint-Simon's writings, the fact emerges that Saint-Sulpice was a modest, practical, and submissive Community, that it stood in awe of the Court, and was powerless because it lacked patronage, and that in cleaving to this Society, Fénelon had probably obeyed, in a far greater measure, his ingrained feelings of grateful affection, rather than any motives based upon niceties of doctrine or calculations of ambition.

We will not say that nothing in Saint-Simon's portrait, or in his remarks, is to be received. These are of service to us, in this one respect at least, that they bid us not to accept in its entirety the Fénelon of legend, and not to consider him exclusively as a saint and an angel, as people are often wont to do. There was something human in this angelic soul ; we would almost venture to admit that we love him only the better for it ; we are more in sympathy with the saints who have sinned, than with those who have not. He was ambitious : "Doubtless every man is," says Voltaire's *Mahomet*. He did not eschew all subtlety, and even perhaps intrigue. In his great conflict with Bossuet, he exhibited as much resourcefulness as tenacity. In a word, he was human. Nevertheless, we believe him to have been incapable of sacrificing his conscience to his fortune. We have a proof of this in his unswerving, although not very reasonable, attachment for Mme. Guyon.

That was the rock upon which his fortune was stranded ; he had enough discernment to perceive the fact. He ought to have abandoned this unhappy woman ; he could have done so ; no one would have reproached him for such a course. One may even consider that his obstinate fidelity to a person whom we regard to-day as half insane, disfigures somewhat the noble personage whom she deluded ; but that is precisely the reason why we see Fénelon to have been so far superior to all considerations of policy, that he did not even sacrifice to mere common sense and regard for his dignity, an undertaking which he believed to be a duty, namely, the defence of persecuted innocence. But we are encroaching too much upon the future. We must return to our starting-point, Fénelon's arrival at Court.

The young Duke of Burgundy, son of His Royal Highness, the Dauphin, had reached an age when it was necessary to think of his education. However severe one may be towards Louis XIV in general, one cannot reproach him with having neglected the education of his children and grandchildren. In the case of the Dauphin, he had appointed Montausier to be his Governor, and Bossuet his Tutor; inspired by the same spirit, he chose for the Duke of Burgundy, Beauvillier and Fénelon. But the education of the Dauphin had proved rather unfruitful; the soil was unpromising. His Royal Highness was by nature apathetic and unimpressionable. He was destined to produce nothing. The Duke of Burgundy, on the other hand, was of a violent and sensitive nature, and in a high degree open to receive impressions from a superior mind. Fénelon has alluded to these two types of character in a passage quoted above.[1]

Saint-Simon, in his delineation of the character of the Duke of Burgundy, gives us to understand what obstacles Fénelon had to overcome in his education : " The Duke of Burgundy was born terrible, and in his early youth he made everyone tremble. Hard and irascible to the utmost passion, incapable of bearing the slightest resistance without flying into a rage which made people fear that his physical frame would entirely give way—all these states I myself have often witnessed ; obstinate to excess, passionately fond of every kind of pleasure, of good food, of hunting with fury, and of

[1] *Cf.* p. 33, *supra.*

music with a sort of rapture. Intellect
and penetration sparkled from him on every
side ; his repartees astonished ; his replies
always tended towards correctness and depth ;
the most abstract knowledge was child's
play to him."

Such was the youth who had to be made
a man of. The exertions of the Duke of
Beauvillier and Fénelon succeeded in this
task to a degree which may well appear
incredible. " The marvel is," continues
Saint-Simon, " that in a very short space
of time, devotion and grace made quite
another being of him, and changed his many
and dreadful faults into the entirely opposite
virtues. From this abyss a Prince was seen
to issue, at once affable, gentle, humane,
generous, patient, modest, humble, and
severe towards himself. Henceforth, he
thought only of combining his duties, as son
and subject, with those to which he saw
himself destined."

We possess an account of one of these
scenes, which reveals the violent character
of the young Prince, as well as the noble
and winning art which Fénelon employed
to bend his unruly nature. It was especially
to the young Prince's sensibility, and to his

generosity that he appealed. On one occasion, Fénelon had blamed him very severely. The young man was indignant, and, alleging his dignity and birth, replied to his Tutor : " No, sir, I know who I am, and who you are." Fénelon did not answer, but spoke to him no more and seemed extremely unhappy. The next morning, Fénelon called on the Duke of Burgundy, and, replying to the insolent offence of the day before, said : " I have no hesitation in telling you that I am more than you. It is not a question now of birth. You cannot dispute the fact that I am greater than you in the matter of wisdom and knowledge ; you know only what I have taught you, and that is nothing compared with what I have yet to teach you. In so far as authority is concerned, you have none over me ; as for me, on the contrary, I have full and complete authority over you. Perhaps you imagine that I consider myself exceedingly fortunate in being entrusted with the functions which I fulfil in connection with you. Be under no misapprehension, your Highness ; I accepted them merely in order to obey the King ; and, in order that you may have no doubt about the matter, I will now conduct you before His Majesty, and request him to appoint another Tutor, in the hope that his endeavours on your behalf may be more successful than mine." The Duke of Burgundy was overwhelmed by this state- ment. He wept and entreated. Fénelon took a day to relent, and appeared to yield only to the entreaties of Mme. de Maintenon.

This dignified and gentle method suc- ceeded remarkably well ; perhaps, as some think, even too well. Fénelon, in giving free scope to the pleasure of mastering so violent a nature, did not perceive that he was breaking its mainsprings. The Duke of Burgundy did not subsequently become the hero he early promised to be. At a later date, Fénelon, then Archbishop of Cambrai, had cause to censure him again, but from an entirely different point of view.[1] He reproached him for his weakness of character, and his excessive tendency to allow himself to be led by others. He also remonstrated with him for his over-scrupulous religious devotion. One is struck by the haughty and imperious tone in which he addressed him. He still seemed to regard

[1] *Cf.* Letters to the Duke of Burgundy, 24 Sept., and 15 Oct., 1708 (*Correspondance*, i, pp. 237 and 252).

him as nothing more than a child and a pupil, although he was then a general in the army. This was not the way to strengthen his will. It is a question whether Fénelon, if he had become Prime Minister, would have proved a pleasant associate for the Sovereign. We are of opinion that Louis XIV, even when a young man, would never have allowed himself to be spoken to in such a manner. But responsibility develops men, and none can tell exactly what the Duke of Burgundy would have done if he had ever been called upon to bear the burden and honour of royalty.

So much for education. As for instruction, Fénelon was not directly concerned with it. Abbé Fleury [1] was entrusted with that, under Fénelon's superintendence. Here are two syllabuses found among Abbé Fleury's papers, and written entirely in Fénelon's hand :

1695. " I think the Duke of Burgundy should be allowed to continue, during the remainder of this year, his compositions and translations, as he is doing them at present.

" The compositions are taken from Ovid's *Metamorphoses ;* the subject offers much

[1] *Cf.* Note xviii, p. 265.

variety ; it teaches him a great number of Latin words and idiomatic expressions ; it amuses him, and, since composition is a most thorny study, as much amusement as possible should be introduced into it.

" The translations are alternately from one of the comedies of Terentius, and from one of the books of the Odes of Horace ; he enjoys them immensely, and nothing could be more profitable either from the point of view of his Latin, or of the development of his taste."

They were much perplexed over the choice of reading books. Fénelon advised Bulteau's *Histoire monastique.*[1] He was also to be made to read the *De Re rustica* of Cato and Columella, the *Georgics*, Cordemoy's *Histoire,*[2] " and portions of the works of our historians. . . . These writers are ridiculous enough to amuse him." A curious incentive to the reading of them ! Finally, he recommended Abbé Fleury's *Histoire d'Angleterre.*

The following year, the Prince's reading was to be of a higher order. Fénelon advocated the Scriptures, and in particular the Wisdom books, a selection of the Letters of the Fathers, Saint Jerome, Saint Augustine,

[1] *Cf.* Note xix, p. 265. [2] *Cf.* Note xx, p. 265.

Saint Cyprian, and Saint Ambrose : "Saint Augustine's *Confessions* possess great charm, in that they are full of varied descriptions and tender feeling." Here we see Fénelon's fondness for the romantic, for the *Confessions* are a veritable romance, and no less disturbing than many a novel.

A noteworthy feature of this scheme of study is the paucity of modern French books then available for the education of youth. Fénelon rightly recommended the reading of history, but there were no good historians. Nothing could be more scanty or incomplete than such a course of reading.

This lack of good books caused Fénelon, as Bossuet had done, to write some himself, and thus it came about that these educational needs had important results for literature. But, whereas the works which Bossuet wrote for this purpose, his *Histoire universelle*, his *Connaissance de Dieu et de soi-même*, are great books, which appeal to men and women, and transcend the limits of their original object, those of Fénelon have remained books designed for education. Some, namely, the *Fables*, are intended for children ; others, the *Dialogues des Morts*, for adolescence and youth. And yet, although they were written from the point of view of education, they have retained in themselves an enduring value, owing to the fine qualities of composition and style which distinguish them.

Fénelon's *Fables* have the drawback of being written in prose, instead of in verse, and this causes them to be less readily committed to memory than verse Fables, for example, those of La Fontaine and even of Florian ; moreover, poetry always possesses greater charm than prose. They are also notably inferior to those of La Fontaine in those rare qualities which place this fabulist in the front rank of our great poets. You will find in Fénelon, neither that magnificent descriptive power, nor that profound philosophic outlook, nor that portrayal of character and passion, nor that native simplicity and originality of style, which make La Fontaine a writer unique in the French language. Still, in spite of all, Fénelon's *Fables* are to be classed among the best ever written. They have a pleasant and cheerful colouring, and are adapted to the minds of children ; they possess wit and feeling, and their style is delightful, and suffused with grace and sweetness.

FÉNELON AS TUTOR

It should be noticed that under the heading of *Fables*, all kinds of literary composition, of very varying character, have been collected. For example, they comprise : 1st, veritable fairy tales : *Histoire d'une vieille reine et d'une jeune paysanne ; Histoire de la reine Gisèle et de la fée Corréante ; Histoire de Florise ; Histoire de Rosimond et de Braminte ;* —2nd, poetic and romantic episodes, similar to those in *Télémaque*, e.g. : *Aventures de Mélésichton ; Aventures d'Aristonoüs ;*—3rd, short stories, such as the charming *Histoire d'Alybée ;*—4th, allegories, e.g. : *Voyage dans l'île des Plaisirs*. The *Fables*, properly so called, are not more than about twenty in number. The following are among the most attractive :

In *l'Abeille et la Mouche*, Fénelon contrasts violence and pride, as represented in the bee, with poverty and simplicity, as personified in the fly. The words of the poor fly are touching : " We live as best we can," replied the fly ; " poverty is not a vice, but anger is, and a great one, too. You make honey, which is sweet, but your heart is always bitter ; you are wise in your laws, but hasty in your actions. Your anger, which stings your enemies, causes your death, and your stupid cruelty is more harmful to yourself than to anyone else."

In the fable entitled *les Deux Renards*, Fénelon sets the miserly prudence of old age in opposition to the thoughtless lack of restraint of youth. " The one, who was young and violent, wanted to devour the whole ; the other, who was old and niggardly, wished to put some by as a provision for the future. . . . The young one eats until he kills himself . . . ; the old one, who thinks he is wiser, desires to return to his prey on the morrow, and is slaughtered by the owner."

Le Jeune Bacchus et le Faune is addressed directly to the Duke of Burgundy. An old Faun derides the youthful Bacchus : " How dare you," says the latter, in haughty and impatient tones, " how dare you make fun of the son of Jupiter ? "—The Faun, nothing daunted, replies : " Ha ! and how should the son of Jupiter dare to be at fault ? "

The fable *le Rossignol et la Fauvette* is an idyll, a graceful lyric poem, rather than a real fable. These two singing birds praise the merits of the young Prince, and imagine him to be, if not what he is, at least what he ought to be. Philomel says : " Let this

young hero grow in virtue, like a flower
which the spring causes to bloom! May
he love the quiet occupations of the mind!
May the graces dwell on his lips! May the
wisdom of Minerva reign in his heart!"
The warbler replies: "Let him equal
Orpheus by the charm of his voice, and
Hercules by his high deeds! May he be
as stout-hearted as Achilles, though not as
fierce! May he be good, prudent, generous,
loving towards all men, and beloved of
them!" Then the two inspired birds continue in combined accents: "He loves our
sweet songs: let them enter into his heart
as the dew falls on our sun-parched lawns!
May the gods restrain his ardour, and prosper
him alway! . . . May he usher in the
golden age!" Were these amiable words
mere flattery? [1] No; for we know that
Fénelon did not spoil his pupil; but they
set before him an embellished picture of
himself, in order to inspire him with the
desire, and to impart to him the strength,
to attain to the reality of the picture.

The *Dialogues des Morts* belong to that
ingenious and attractive literary form be-
queathed to us by the Ancients, in which

[1] *Cf.* Note xxi, p. 266.

FÉNELON

Lucian was past-master. The latter had
made use of it, so to speak, as a substitute
for the satire. Fénelon employs it as a
vehicle for education. At every step allusions to the Duke of Burgundy are to be
found. In the Dialogue *Mercure et Charon*,
the former, speaking of the young Prince,
expresses himself in the following terms :
" I think he will love peace and will know
how to wage war. The promise of a great
Prince is discernible in him, just as one sees
in a growing rose-bud what promises to be
a beautiful flower. . . . He is impetuous,
but not unkind ; he is inquiring, gentle,
full of appreciation for lovely things. . . .
If he can overcome his hastiness and his
laziness, he will be marvellous.—What !
hasty and lazy, these things are contra-
dictory !—No ; he is quickly angered, and
lax in the performance of his tasks, but
every day he improves."—In the Dialogue
Chiron et Achille, the question of the fiery
temperament of the young Prince is again
raised : " Youth is a strange malady ; it
would be a charming age if its exuberance
could be moderated. You, to whom so
many remedies are known, have you none
to cure this impetuosity, this heat of the

blood, more dangerous than a burning fever ? "—In the Dialogue *Achille et Homère*, he shows the way to arouse in the heart of a young Prince, a love of polite learning and glory, and he shows us what a hero owes to a great poet.

The principal subject-matter of the *Dialogues* is not merely ethics in general, as in the *Fables*, but ethics applied to politics. The Dialogue *Romulus et Rémus* is a kind of refutation of Machiavelli.[1] It teaches us that greatness obtained by crime is incapable of yielding either pleasure or lasting happiness ; *Romulus et Tatius* shows that true heroism is incompatible with violence and deceit, and *Romulus et Numa*, that the glory of a peaceful king is more to be desired than that of a conqueror. It may be said that these are only common-places : yes, if the Dialogues were addressed to us, who, over and over again, have heard these great and familiar moral truths ; but they cease to be common-places when one remembers that the question at issue was the upbringing of a Prince, who was to be King of France, and to succeed Louis XIV. To prefer peace to war, meekness to violence,

[1] *Cf.* Note xxii, p. 266.

and good faith to duplicity, is a complete political programme ; it is the formulation and foreshadowing of a change in the system of government. There is, therefore, something more than rhetorical display in this Dialogue.

The same observations apply to the following Dialogue, *Pisistrate et Solon :* that tyranny is more disastrous to the sovereign than to the people. In *Socrate et Alcibiade,* we find sentiments of humanity and liberalism, which are foreign to the age of Fénelon, and which forestall Montesquieu : " Does not the slavery of the helots appear to you contrary to humanity ? . . . Is it permissible for one section of men to treat the other like beasts of burden ? . . . Subject peoples still remain human beings. . . . Every man owes infinitely more to the human race, which is the great fatherland, than to the little fatherland in which he was born." And everywhere the same objurgations against war : [1] " War is an evil which dishonours mankind. . . . All wars are civil wars, for they are always between man and man." Finally, Fénelon recommends the sovereignty of law : " The one

[1] *Cf.* Note xxiii, p. 266.

who governs ought to be the most obedient to the law."—Away with absolute monarchy : " The Persians placed themselves in such a state of slavery under those who ought to encourage the reign of law, that the latter rule in their own persons, and there is no longer any real law save their absolute will." Another Dialogue, *Dion et Gélon*, is devoted to the following maxim, renewed from antiquity : " It is not man that should reign, but the laws."—" Man must not govern ; he must be content to ensure the omnipotence of the laws ; if he arrogates to himself the sovereign power, he corrupts it and ruins himself." In the Dialogue, *César et Caton*, it is proved that absolute power, far from ensuring the tranquillity and authority of Princes, is a source of misfortune to them, and leads to their ruin." We shall meet with these maxims again in *Télémaque*, and in Fénelon's views on statecraft. What stands out most prominently in this educational course is aversion for, and condemnation of, absolutism : and it was at the Court of Louis XIV, in his presence, and for the benefit of his grandson, that these political conceptions were enunciated ! Nothing proves better the liberty and independence which were granted to Fénelon in his delicate functions; the stumbling-block in his career was not here; he found it elsewhere, and we have now to relate the great crisis of his life.[1]

[1] *Cf.* Note xxiv, p. 267.

CHAPTER IV

FÉNELON AND MADAME GUYON

Two women exercised a supreme influence on Fénelon's career, and each had a share in bringing his fortune to a standstill: Mme. Guyon and Mme. de Maintenon, who, after being friends, became enemies.

It would be difficult to imagine two women more unlike each other. The one seems to be the incarnation of reason, the other verges on insanity. Mme. Guyon lives only the inner life, and regards all outward occurrences as naught; Mme. de Maintenon lives only for the world's esteem, and temporal duties outweigh all others. The one was imprisoned and died unremembered; the other became a Queen and enjoyed a life of splendour. Despite so many differences, there must have been some points of agreement between them, seeing they were fond of each other for a time, and had a mutual friend. The reason is that Mme. de Maintenon, in spite of all that is said about her harshness and cold reason, had a tinge of Mysticism. She had a profound contempt

for the people to whom she owed everything ; she hated life, although it had been
so prosperous for her ; she needed to love
and take refuge in God. Hence the attraction she experienced for the society of Fénelon
and Mme. Guyon. The latter, on the other
hand, who, in her Autobiography,[1] proves
herself to be the very antithesis of cold
reason, being all enthusiasm, ecstacy, and
love, had also her secular and worldly side.
She was fond of pleasing, and she knew
how to please. How can we believe that,
in the distinguished and enlightened company of such men as Beauvillier and Chevreuse, at Saint-Cyr,[2] in the presence of
Mme. de Maintenon, or before Fénelon himself, she should have begun by making herself known with all those hysterical excesses and eccentricities, which were later
to revolt Bossuet ? Doubtless, with the
cunning familiar to neurotic women, she
knew how to obliterate or hide what might
have appeared ridiculous or odious. She
retained her mystical phraseology, but without compromising herself in the eyes of the
world. Her conversation must have been

[1] *Cf.* Note xxv, p. 268.

[2] *Cf.* Note xxvi, p. 268.

fascinating and bewitching. Something of its charm remains in her writings. Her *Moyen court* and her *Torrents* are written in a brilliant and dignified style, which is not devoid of a certain measure of precision, as much as is compatible with absolute vagueness of subject-matter. In order to have gained over Fénelon to the point of unreasonable obstinacy, and to have captivated Mme. de Maintenon, she must have made herself appear more rational than she really was. Mme. de Maintenon, on the contrary, was, perhaps, less reasonable at bottom than she appeared to be, and this accounts for her fascination. Yet, when the critical moment came for her to choose between an independent form of piety and the official faith, and, above all, when she saw her credit and power compromised by dangerous acquaintances, she was once again what she had always been, level-headed, reasonable, calculating, and self-denying.

Who then was this Mme. Guyon, who was the cause of so great a disturbance at the close of the seventeenth century, who set the Court and the Church ablaze, and caused the greatest Prelates of the age to fall out, and whose name has become inseparable from Fénelon's ? She was born at Montargis in 1648, of a family of petty nobility, the de la Mothes. She was sickly from birth, and was taken for dead on several occasions : this fact caused her baptism to be deferred. She was very much neglected by her mother, although the latter was, according to her daughter's own testimony, extremely religious and charitable. But her virtues did not prevent her abandoning her daughter to the care of servants, and concentrating all her affection on her son. What degree of credence are we to place upon Mme. Guyon in the exceedingly severe accusations which she brings to bear on her parents' conduct towards her, as well as on her husband, and her mother-in-law, while at the same time extolling their virtues ? Her over-excitable imagination may have made her see everywhere around her ill-will or neglect, which was of a less serious nature than she supposed. Her nervous system inclined her to an insane belief that she was the butt of persecution. Be that as it may, she was brought up at a Convent by an elder sister for whom she always manifested a great fondness. On her return to her family, she regained the affection of her mother, who began to be proud of her beauty and intelligence, for she does not leave us in ignorance of the fact that she was endowed with both. She had deplorably bad health, and was several times attacked by extraordinary maladies. She was scarcely more than twelve or fourteen years of age, when they began to talk of marrying her, and she was introduced to several persons who, by birth and outward accomplishments, might have suited her. Unfortunately her parents, on the look out for wealth before all else, handed her over, at the age of fifteen, to a Mr. Guyon, who was twenty years her senior, a gouty person, who spent the greater part of his time in bed, and to whom she became a nurse rather than a wife. He was also, if we are to accept the evidence of his wife, a man of violent and brutal disposition, and much beneath her, not only from the point of view of intellect, but also of birth and manners. Thus it was that, at a time when the family spirit is by some supposed to have been so highly developed, they married a girl without consulting her, and without her having any knowledge of her husband (she first saw him two days only before her marriage), but solely for money, since there was not even the attraction of a great name, and that in a Christian family! If we are to believe Mme. Guyon, she had much to suffer not only from her husband's temper, but also from that of her mother-in-law, which was even more violent ; this woman appears to have behaved as a veritable termagant towards her : it was a never-ending persecution. To fill up the measure, one of the maid-servants of the house, who was of a jealous and hypocritical turn of mind, never ceased, for her part, to treat her violently, and to humiliate and insult her in a most odious fashion, meanwhile complaining to her masters of the supposed ill-treatment she herself was receiving at the hands of her mistress. Her home life was a hell to Mme. Guyon. She had no other consolation save religion. Throughout her childhood, she had been pious, and had even desired to become a nun. Yet she was not content with the ordinary practices of devotion. The outward acts of religion, confession, prayer, Communion even, were powerless either to overcome her faults, of which the two chief were anger and pride, or to comfort her in her griefs. But one day she met a nun, who revealed to her the mystery of a higher life, and taught her how to pray (*faire oraison*). From that day she was saved and her doctrine established. What then is prayer ? She does not tell us in her Autobiography ; but we shall learn from her writings. We may say here that, in her eyes, prayer is a simple and indistinct act, by which the soul yields itself up to God, without words or any clear conceptions, an act which, according to the mystics, takes the place of ordinary religious observances. From that time onward, the " prayer of quiet " became habitual with Mme. Guyon ; but it was a new subject of dissension and persecution in her family. Her husband, her mother-in-law, and the favourite old servant, could neither understand, nor endure, these self-surrenders, silences, and ecstacies, which were substituted for the positive and definite religious practices required of ordinary believers. They would not allow her to retire to her room ; they were angry with her when she remained silent, although previously they had reproached her for talking too much and striving to be witty. However, nothing availed ; and notwithstanding all that was done, and in spite of everybody, in the midst of her family and even in society, she contrived to indulge in the " prayer of quiet." But the inner evil, sin, was not yet entirely uprooted ; it would constantly return. Particularly when she went to Paris, she would give herself up to vanity again. She was very glad to be thought pleasing, and would go to the Cours[1] in order to be seen ; she still wore too low-necked dresses, although much less so than was the prevailing fashion. She admitted that " she hated passions in so far as she herself was concerned, but that she did not hate exciting them in others." Such weaknesses have holy women ! Saint Teresa relates that, in her early days, she had little meetings in secret with young men, and that she allowed herself to be kissed by them ; but this was before her sainthood. In the case of Mme. Guyon, saintliness did not as yet protect her wholly from the vanity of the world, although, as a matter of fact, there was never anything blameworthy in her conduct. Despite all the efforts subsequently made to prove her guilt, absolutely nothing contrary to morals has ever been detected in

[1] *Cf.* Note xxvii, p. 270.

her life.[1] Perhaps, however, she was proof against this species of sin owing to insensibility, for she tells us that her soul and body were distinctly separate, that "her body did things as though it did them not. I think I speak with sufficient clearness to make myself understood." It is true that these are precisely the kind of divisions of the self which have led certain mystics to believe themselves innocent of everything which took place in the region of the body, and to imagine that saintliness when once acquired could never again be lost, whatever the actions which might happen to be done in the body. But Mme. Guyon never taught this doctrine.[2]

Meanwhile many bodily ties still remained, and she made astonishing efforts to mortify her senses. For this purpose she would condescend to the most repulsive, and, in a word, the most degrading acts. Her states, which she calls spiritual, appear to have been, in certain cases, nervous states analagous to those which we find in hysterical women to day. Of this description is the following passage, culled by Bossuet

[1] *Cf.* Note xxviii, p. 270.
[2] *Cf.* Note xxix, p. 271.

from the manuscript Autobiography which she had entrusted to him, but which does not figure in the printed Autobiography. She claimed to possess the power of diffusing spiritual grace around her : " Those who are close to me," she wrote, " are inwardly nourished with the grace communicated by me in plenitude. . . . I felt by degrees emptied and relieved. . . . It was like a terrific discharge of lightning, others felt themselves replenished, while I felt eased." She was " like a wet-nurse bursting with milk." She added : "I am apparently in a bare and vacuous condition, nevertheless, I was very replete. When water fills a basin, the abundance of it can in no wise be distinguished so long as the water remains within the limits of the capacity of the basin ; but if a surplus amount be added, the basin must discharge itself or burst." One might imagine that she was dealing in metaphors only : unfortunately Mme. Guyon spoke literally, and went so far as to burst in the non-figurative sense of the word. " It was during one of these paroxysms of plenitude," says Bossuet, " that upon one occasion, being in the company of several persons, she told them she was dying of plenitude, and that this influx so overflowed her senses that she must needs burst." This was the time the Duchess of Béthune " unlaced me," she says, " spite of which my body burst on both sides, on account of the violence of this plenitude." [1] She also went so far as to claim the gifts of prophecy and miracle, if we are to believe Bossuet, who had sight of the manuscript Autobiography ; from the printed version, however, these illusions, which border too closely on heresy, seem to have been expurgated.

The principal events in her life, entirely devoted to piety, are illnesses, pregnancy, and the intermittences of piety and indifference ; an account of these things is to be found in her Autobiography. Suffice it to say, that she gave birth successively to four children, and that she lost the eldest girl through small-pox. She gives us no details concerning them, and we shall see further on how far she carried her indifference towards them.

Before long Mme. Guyon's life was completely changed. She lost her husband after having nursed him as a Sister of Mercy might have done. She had to attend to the

[1] Cf. Note xxx, p. 271.

somewhat complicated matters relating to the estate ; and she was astonished herself at the ease with which she became acquainted with things hitherto unfamiliar to her. At this juncture she gave evidence of that aptitude for affairs which has often been noted among the mystics.[1] Her husband's death did not render her mother-in-law more sociable. The latter continued to annoy and harass her in every way, until finally they were obliged to part company. After the separation had taken place, the mother-in-law returned to more reasonable feelings ; she appears to have realised, at last, the merits of her daughter-in-law, and she made amends for all the wrongs she had inflicted upon her.

Then came an eclipse, lasting a few years, in Mme. Guyon's religious vocation. She fell into that state of spiritual torpor which the mystics have so often described. We do not quite know wherein these infidelities consisted. She said everyone was blaming her, and that she had forfeited her reputation. It is not in the least likely that her fall from grace had anything to do with a lapse from morals, but only with a slackness

[1] *Cf.* Note xxxi, p. 272.

in religious devotion, especially in its outward manifestations. She no longer went to Church as heretofore, nor had she the holy inspirations of the devout life. This state of spiritual apathy came to an end as a result of her meeting with a man who was destined to exercise a great influence upon her life, Father Lacombe. She furnishes us with very few details about this person, who appears rather to have been initiated by her into the mystical life than to have opened it up to her. At all events there existed, from the outset, a remarkable agreement of sentiment and will between these two souls, which, even at a distance, continued to commune in the spirit. She was then in such a strange state of mind that the dogmas of religion seem to have become matters of indifference to her, and that for a while she even entertained the idea of becoming a Protestant ; she resisted the temptation, but it was doubtless this short-lived design that prompted the singular inspiration which was to change her whole life, namely, the decision to leave her family and go to Geneva. Why Geneva ? She does not tell us : she seems to have obeyed a kind of auto-suggestion, similar to those which have been so admirably studied in our own time in cases of hysteria. She wrote, therefore, to the Bishop of Geneva to inform him of her intention. The latter, who was delighted to know that so saintly and wealthy a woman was about to arrive in his diocese, tried to direct his correspondent's worthy impulse towards a definite object. There was at that time, in the district of Geneva, a Convent of Sisters, known under the name of *Nouvelles Catholiques*, with a branch in Paris. They were Protestant young women who had recently been converted to Roman Catholicism. We have seen how Fénelon had been appointed Chaplain to the Convent in Paris. To this overture on the part of the Genevan prelate, Mme. Guyon, who was never disposed to set to work with a clear end in view, sent a stiff reply containing an extraordinary excuse to the effect that these Sisters were not at Geneva, but at Gex (which is quite close to Geneva), and that the inspiration from on High which had come to her had reference to Geneva only. In the meantime, she communicated with the Sisters in Paris, but with no other result than to convince herself still further that that was not at all what she needed. And, as a matter of fact, knowing her as we do, the change from one dogma to another, from Protestantism to Roman Catholicism, must have struck her as of very little importance in comparison with the true religious life, which, in her estimate, was so vastly superior to both. Meanwhile her resolution remained unshaken ; she spoke to everyone about it. All level-headed people warned her against it, as against an out-of-the-way and unreasonable thing. On the other hand, her mystic correspondents, particularly Father Lacombe, urged her to listen to the voice of God. She therefore made up her mind and set out with her daughter, aged five, abandoning her two other children, and thenceforth troubling no more about them : her notions respecting family ties were on a level with those of Orgon.[1] This neglect of maternal duties was one of the things with which she was most reproached at a later time, although Bossuet, who frequently treated her with great severity, never mentioned this incident ; it is surprising how a man of Fénelon's loving nature could have been misled by mystical theories to the point of allowing himself to be beguiled by

[1] *Cf.* Note xxxii, p. 272.

so unreasonable a woman, who was capable of sacrificing the most sacred duties to a supposed state of perfection, of which she constituted herself the sole judge, and which was nothing but the disordered conception of her own imagination. So she set out, and, with characteristic inconsistency, took up her abode with those very *Nouvelles Catholiques*, with whom she had at first proclaimed herself quite unable to agree. She remained with them for several months ; the Bishop offered to appoint her their Superior, but she refused to act contrary to the rule of the Convent by accepting to become Superior without having first been a novice. In reality she had too much independence of mind to endure the servitude of the religious life. At the same time, in order to sever herself completely from the world, she put in order her private affairs, surrendered her fortune to her heirs, doubtless reserving her children's rights, and contenting herself with a life-annuity. After having deprived herself of her fortune, she does not appear to have been the object of the same attentions on the part of the Bishop and the nuns ; at all events she cut herself off from them and went to live in the country with her little daughter. Then it was that an incident happened, which she terms a miracle, but which is now entirely accounted for by present-day science. For several months she had had a persistent cough, which nothing availed to relieve. Father Lacombe merely had to say to her : " Cough no more," for the cough to cease as by enchantment. In this miracle we discover to-day a proof of her hysterical tendencies : for the above is one of the most characteristic instances of suggestion which she relates, manifestly without understanding it. [1]

From this time onwards Mme. Guyon led a merely wandering and aimless life. She went to Turin, Grenoble, Marseilles, Alexandria, Genoa, and Vercelli. She never once asked herself the purpose subserved by the heavenly inspiration which had urged her to proceed to Geneva, where she had remained hardly more than a day. She had fallen out with the *Nouvelles Catholiques*, with the Ursulines, and with the Bishop of Geneva on account of her so-called revelations. All kinds of things were said against her and her spiritual director, Father

[1] *Cf.* Note xxxiii, p. 273.

Lacombe, concerning whom innumerable rumours were current. It was said she had ridden on a horse behind him, or in the same coach which had capsized. Everyone was against her; but now and again she would meet with a devout soul, who welcomed her and fed on her words. At Grenoble, more than elsewhere, she exercised a kind of apostolate. She was at home from six in the morning till eight at night; but her fame soon caused her to be expelled from Grenoble. Finally, after numerous adventures, too long to narrate, but worthy of a novel, she decided to return to Paris with Father Lacombe: five years had elapsed since her departure from France. It was now that she was destined to experience more serious persecutions.

All kinds of sorry imputations against Mme. Guyon and her spiritual director, either on the score of doctrine or of private conduct, had obtained currency before their arrival in Paris. The leading spirit in this cabal, according to Mme. Guyon herself, was her own brother, Father de la Mothe, who was jealous, on the one hand, of Father Lacombe's success as a preacher, and furious, on the other, at not having had his share of his sister's possessions when she had bestowed them all upon her relatives. Father Lacombe had been placed in the Bastille ; his penitent was shut up in the Convent of the Visitation of the Rue Saint-Antoine. The intervention of Mme. de Miramion, one of the most saintly women in Paris, who is also known for her extraordinary adventures, put an end to this imprisonment. Mme. de Miramion was on excellent terms with Mme. de Maintenon ; the latter, in turn, became interested in Mme. Guyon, pleaded her cause with Louis XIV, and obtained her release from the Convent after a captivity which had lasted six months (Sept. 15, 1688). She then entered upon a period of glory and triumph. It was at this time that she made the acquaintance of Fénelon.

Fénelon, as Chaplain of the Convent of the *Nouvelles Catholiques*, must have heard of Mme. Guyon when she made her first application for admission to the Convent. Having had occasion to visit Montargis, he had again heard her spoken of in that place as a saint. Then, after her release from captivity, when she was welcomed by all the most distinguished representatives of the pious circles of Paris, she met at first some of Fénelon's lady friends ; shortly afterwards she met Fénelon himself : " He saw her," says Saint-Simon, " their minds pleased each other ; their *sublime* amalgamated." [1] The first meeting took place at the house of the Duchess of Béthune, in the country. Fénelon returned to Paris in a coach with Mme. Guyon, accompanied by one of the Duchess's attendants. One cannot sufficiently admire the ease with which saints of both sexes place themselves in delicate situations. No doubt there was a witness ; but several hours of conversation on pure love, between two persons still young, and as remarkable for their beauty as for their intelligence, are not without some danger. However, Mme. Guyon herself tells us of her first meeting with Fénelon : " I was suddenly taken up with him most forcibly and delightfully. It seemed to me as though Our Lord were uniting him to me in a most intimate manner and more than any other." Yet the attraction was not at once mutual : " I felt," she says, " that our first interview did not gratify him, and that I was not appreciated ; as for me, I felt an indescribable something, which tended to make me

[1] *Cf.* Note xxxiv, p. 274.

pour out my heart into his, but I found that this was in no wise reciprocated. . . . I suffered eight whole days, after which I found myself united to him without impediment." Soon the charm became all powerful : " He was led away," says d'Aguesseau, " like the first man, by the voice of a woman ; his gifts, his fortune, his very reputation were sacrificed, not to the delusions of the senses, but to those of the mind." [1]

Mme. Guyon was introduced by Mme. de Béthune and Fénelon to the little circle of the Beauvilliers and Chevreuses, with which Mme. de Maintenon was on familiar terms. She was admitted into the private gatherings where matters of pietism were discussed, and she herself spoke at these meetings with the charm and fascination which distinguished her. Mme. de Maintenon never wearied of listening to her, as she talked of the love of God. She read passages from the *Moyen court*, even before Louis XIV, who said her ideas were " dreams." This was the very time when fortune, smiling on Fénelon, was summoning him to become the Tutor of a Prince (1689). Thus, his early relations with Mme. Guyon were in no wise prejudicial

[1] *Cf.* Note xxxv, p. 274.

to him. He was the director of a little court
of devout persons, whither Mme. de Maintenon would retire to rest from the Court
of Louis XIV. These little pietistic gatherings were held at Marly, and Mme. Guyon
was invited to them. They hearkened to
her as to an oracle. At this time she published her *Cantique des Cantiques*, a bold
commentary on the *Moyen court* and the
Torrents. Saint-Cyr itself was not secure
from the mystical influences of Mme. Guyon.
She had a cousin there, Mlle. de la Maisonfort,
who was as enthusiastic as herself. She
had taken the part of Elise in the tragedy
of *Esther*.[1] Mme. de Maintenon, who had
opened the doors of Saint-Cyr to poetry
and the drama, did not guard the establishment against the allurements of religious
devotion : "Mme. Guyon charmed our ladies
with her intelligence and her pious discourses.
She gave her books to be read, and ere long
her doctrine seemed the way to perfection."
Fénelon was put in touch with Mlle. de la
Maisonfort, and he had his share in that
gentle coercion which was brought to bear
upon her, and which led her, almost in spite
of herself, to take her vows. From that

[1] *Cf.* Note xxvi, p. 269.

time she became an apostle : " Nearly the whole of the establishment turned quietist ; they talked about nought save pure love and holy indifference ; instead of doing their work, [1] the lay sisters spent their time reading Mme. Guyon's books." The indiscretion of Mlle. de la Maisonfort, who, in spite of Fénelon's advice, showed these books to everybody, brought about the crisis which had long threatened. Fénelon's error of judgment was visited upon him. He had made a nun of Mlle. de la Maisonfort in spite of herself ; it was her own over-zealous display of devotion that proved the undoing both of Mme. Guyon, and of Fénelon himself. This is how the crisis is related by Saint-Simon. According to his version, Fénelon's desire was to supplant Godet, the Bishop of Chartres, as Mme. de Maintenon's religious director.

" He was," says Saint-Simon, " an odd rival to overthrow, but however well anchored he might be, his external appearance, which was that of a vulgar pedant, reassured him (Fénelon). He believed him to be really such, from his long, squalid, and fleshless face, which was thoroughly Sulpician ; his crude and simple air, and silly appearance,

[1] Cf. Note xxxvi, p. 275.

and his intimacy with none save the inferior priests; in short, he regarded him as a man without connections, without talents, with little sense, and very deficient in knowledge. . . . This prelate was far from being what M. de Cambrai had thought him. He was very learned and, above all, he was a profound theologian. To this he added much wit, gentleness, firmness, and even grace. . . . As soon as he got wind of this strange doctrine, he obtained for two of the ladies of Saint-Cyr, on whose spirit and discretion he could rely, the privilege of being instructed in it. He chose two who were absolutely devoted to him, and instructed them well. These new proselytes seemed at first delighted, then, little by little, bewitched. . . . M. de Chartres, by whose consent Mme. Guyon had entered Saint-Cyr and become a visiting mistress, let her do what she liked. He kept his eye upon her, his faithful pair meanwhile rendering him an exact account of what they were learning as to dogmas and practices. He made himself fully acquainted with everything, he examined the whole matter minutely, and when he thought the time had come, he blazed forth." [1]

[1] *Cf.* Saint-Simon's *Mémoires*, i, p. 303.

FÉNELON AND MADAME GUYON

" Mme. de Maintenon was strangely surprised. She was much troubled and had great qualms. She resolved to speak to M. de Cambrai ; the latter entangled himself in his replies, and increased her suspicions. All of a sudden, Mme. Guyon was expelled from Saint-Cyr. M. de Chartres seized this opportunity of showing the great danger of this poison, and of pouring suspicion upon M. de Cambrai. Such a reverse, so little expected, surprised Fénelon, but did not cast him down. He retaliated with witty sallies, mystical authorities, and firmness in his stirrups ; his principal friends supported him."

Fénelon was not at first involved in the disgrace which had overtaken Mme. Guyon. The proceedings against the latter began in 1693, and Fénelon was appointed Archbishop of Cambrai in 1695. The Conferences of Issy, in which he took part, were also held in 1695. Nothing, therefore, had compromised him up to that date. The crisis did not come till later. Let us now see, from Mme. de Maintenon's own correspondence, what were the different phases of the disaffection and rupture which soon definitely estranged her from Fénelon. She was considerably perplexed. She had greatly loved Fénelon, and had made him her unattached and semi-official spiritual director. She had herself recommended him to Louis XIV for the Archbishopric of Cambrai, and had become friendly with Mme. Guyon on his advice and recommendation. On the other hand, her piety was as strong as it was deep ; she deprecated any departure from the strict rule, and, above all, she dreaded to displease Louis XIV, who was anything but a mystic. She did what she could to defend her friends, but, as soon as the verdict of religious and political leaders was given, she did not hesitate to abandon them. In 1694, she was still protecting Mme. Guyon against Bossuet ; up till 1695, she continued to receive confidential letters from Fénelon, and to praise his sermons ; she would excuse his intentions and his weakness for his friend. " M. de Fénelon," she wrote, " gave me the assurance that he was concerned in this affair only in order to prevent the opinions of the truly religious from being condemned through inadvertence. He is not the advocate of Mme. Guyon, although he is her friend. He is the upholder of Christian piety and perfection.

I rely on his word, because I have known few men as frank as he is." But distrust soon set in : " I have had a great deal of intercourse with M. de Cambrai, but neither of us succeeds in persuading the other. The coolness between these ladies (the Duchesses of Beauvillier and Chevreuse) and myself increases every day." Fénelon alludes to this coldness in a letter of April 6, 1696 : " Why do you close your heart to us, Madam, as though ours were a different religion from yours ? " It was always Mme. Guyon who was the stumbling-block : " I met our friend," says Mme. de Maintenon, in a letter of October 7, " we had a great argument ; . . . would I were as faithful and devoted to my duty as he is to his friends." Then came the publication of the *Maximes des Saints*, of which we shall speak in the next chapter. Mme. de Maintenon keeps us fully informed of the successive phases of the whole business : " M. de Cambrai spoke with me privately for a short time ; he knows the bad impression his book has made, and he defends it on grounds which persuade me more and more that God wills to humiliate this great mind, who has perhaps relied too much on his own wisdom."

Soon after she breaks off entirely with the quietistic party, and she goes so far as to express herself on the matter with a certain amount of harshness : " I see more and more every day, how much I have been misled by all these people, to whom I gave my entire confidence without possessing theirs ; for if they acted with singleness of purpose, why did they not initiate me into their mysteries, and if they feared to reveal them to me, is it not a proof that they had a preconceived design ? " Mme. de Maintenon had indirectly to bear the consequences of the King's displeasure : " He blames me seriously ; the penalty for this affair must fall on me alone." This point marks the termination of the relations of Fénelon with Mme. de Maintenon. From the time of his departure for Cambrai, she saw him no more, nor did she even correspond with him ; she disappeared out of his life, at the same time, in fact, as Mme. Guyon herself, whom Fénelon absolutely ceased to see from that time forth.

Let us return to Mme. Guyon. Now that the time has come when she is about to become the object of an ecclesiastical in-quiry, the results of which will reflect on

Fénelon himself, it is necessary for us to understand the principles of her doctrine ; and, for this purpose, we shall give an analysis of the best and most important of her works, namely : *le Moyen court et très facile de faire oraison*. Her treatise, *les Torrents*, and her Commentary on the *Cantique des Cantiques*, are merely the development of the *Moyen court*.[1]

The essential point in her Mysticism is the definition of prayer. According to Mme. Guyon, prayer (l'oraison) is nothing but " the application of the soul to God." It is an act of love. The prayer referred to is not the prayer of the head, but " of the heart." This state of prayer is admitted by all theologians ; but, whereas they allow that it is only an exceptional state, reserved to the few, the distinctive feature of Mme. Guyon's doctrine is that, according to her, " all are capable of this prayer, to which we are all called, even as we are called to salvation. Let not those who are without love in their hearts come to it ; but who is really devoid of love ? " There are two ways by which the soul may be introduced into

[1] *Cf. Opuscules spirituels de Mme. Guyon* (Cologne, 1704).

the state of prayer : meditation and reading ; even those who are unable to read are not deprived of prayer. Jesus Christ is the great book around us and within. They must learn this fundamental truth that the Kingdom of God is within us. Let them say the Lord's Prayer, remembering that the Kingdom is within them. After uttering the word " Father," let them remain for a few moments in silence and filled with awe. They must not overburden themselves with an inordinate number of *Paters* and vocal prayers. This is the first stage of prayer ; the second is the prayer of simplicity or of *quiet*. As soon as one has experienced a measure of delight in the presence of God, one should remain in that state and not go beyond ; one must gently fan the flames, and cease only when the fire is kindled. The soul must come with a pure and disinterested [1] love, nor must it be troubled because of coldness. Some think they are giving a better proof of love by seeking God with the understanding and by much activity. No ; one must await the return of the Beloved in loving patience, with downcast and humiliated gaze, and in

[1] *Cf.* Note xxxvii, p. 275.

respectful silence. At this point begins the abandonment or gift of the self to God. One must renounce all particular inclinations, however good they may appear, in order to attain holy indifference, in matters pertaining to the soul, to the body, and to all temporal and eternal goods. One must have one's meed of suffering, " the cross in God, and God in the cross." But, it may be objected, " the mysteries will not be imparted thus." On the contrary, " loving attention to God includes all special forms of devotion." " He who is united to God only, because he rests in Him, is excellently attuned to all the mysteries. He who loves God, loves everything that comes from Him." External virtue is nothing : " All virtue which does not originate from within is a lack of virtue. Perfect conversion is not that which goes from sin to grace, although this is better ; it is that which proceeds from without inwards. By the effort which it makes to turn itself entirely within, with no other force save the weight of love, the soul gravitates by degrees into the centre ; the more peaceful and quiet the soul remains, with no motion of its own, the more rapid is its advance." Another degree of prayer is the prayer of the simple presence of God, or active contemplation. In this state, God's presence becomes so easy to realise that it is granted as a result of habit, as well as in response to prayer. One must then allow one's own activity and co-opera-tion to cease, in order to let God work. Those who tax this prayer with idleness are mis-taken ; it is, on the contrary, an act of a superior order. "It is not an unfruitful silence, as of dearth ; it is a plentiful and unctuous silence, as of abundance. A child hanging on the breast begins by moving his tiny lips to cause the milk to rise ; but as soon as there is a full supply of milk, he is content to imbibe it with a uniform motion." In like manner, the presence of God is infused, and is almost continuous during this state. Contrition is prescribed, and quite rightly, for it is indispensable ; but some do not perceive that contrition is precisely this inflowing love, this exalted act which contains all the rest. Let them yield to the working of God and remain silent. God cannot be more worthily re-ceived than by a God. The soul in this state must not overburden itself with vocal prayers ; and if, when it is uttering these, the soul is moved to silence, let it dwell therein. True prayer is the annihilation of self : it is the prayer of truth. These two facts alone subsist : the *All* and the *Nothing*. All else is illusion. Some think that in prayer the soul remains dead, stupefied, and inert ; on the contrary, it is an action, only an action full of quiet, so tranquil, elevated, and peaceful, that the soul appears to be lifeless. The more it is at rest, the faster it runs, because it surrenders itself to the Spirit that impels it. And thus the soul attains to that simplicity and unity in which it was created. The soul becomes one, that is to say identified, with the Spirit of God. What we have to destroy in ourselves is ownership and activity : ownership, because it is the source of real impurity ; activity, because God being in a state of infinite quietude, the soul must participate in His quietude. This is not destroying human liberty ; the soul must give its consent, but a *passive* consent. God so purifies our soul from all personal, distinct, visible, and repeated operations, that at last, and by degrees, He makes it uniform and conformable to Himself, raising the passive capacity of the creature, broadening it, and ennobling it, albeit in a hidden manner, which has, therefore, come to be known as *mystic*. Not that we can dispense with activity altogether, for it is the *gateway*, but we must not remain there.

This is a summary, almost in Mme. Guyon's own words, of the celebrated work *le Moyen court*. However obscure it may be, it gives an idea of the fascination which Mme. Guyon must have had over pious and thoughtful souls, in whom the imagination predominated. Her style, more or less correct, was expressive, picturesque, and original, full of resources to express the inexpressible, elucidate the obscure, give speech to silence, and shed light in darkness. From the doctrinal point of view, it was an attenuated and less extreme form of Quietism, in which traces of an absolute Quietism might be detected. It is especially in the *Torrents*, and in the *Cantique des Cantiques*, that exaggerations are to be discerned. Such was the doctrine [1] which the Bishop of Chartres had discovered at Saint-Cyr, and probably in a much more daring form in those secret conversations. It was these opinions in general that the Bishop of Chartres

[1] *Cf.* Note xxxviii, p. 275.

invited his colleagues in the episcopate to pronounce judgment upon. The commission entrusted with this inquiry was composed of Godet, Bishop of Chartres, Noailles, Archbishop of Paris, and also Bossuet, and Fénelon. It met frequently, and its deliberations were slow and conscientiously circumspect. The outcome of the inquiry was embodied in what are known as the *Articles* of the Conference of Issy (1696). Bossuet and Fénelon were in agreement during the early phases of this affair, which, nevertheless, marks the origin of the dissensions which rapidly developed into a conflict, scandalous for the Church, and disastrous to the fortunes of Fénelon.

CHAPTER V

Now that Bossuet enters upon the scene, we must inquire into the reasons which led such eminent Prelates as the Bishop of Chartres, the Archbishop of Paris, and the Bishop of Meaux, to attach so much importance to the writings and teachings of a society woman, who was not a theologian, and who did not even know how to weigh her words : was it really worth while to set the Church on fire, and, by violent and hardly Christian controversies, to cause a scandal in society, because of too much, or too little Mysticism in a woman ? The saintly Baroness de Chantal, the grandmother of Mme. de Sévigné, had not been troubled in her pious ejaculations ; and was there, after all, such a substantial difference between the one and the other ?

Possibly not ; but the main difference lay in the two periods. In the interval of time which separates Mme. de Chantal from Mme. Guyon, a doctrine had appeared, which, after having been received at first with edification, and later with distrust, had finally incurred a sensational condemnation. This doctrine, known as *Quietism*, had been propounded a few years previously by the Spanish monk Molinos, who, under the guise of an exalted piety, had taught principles of a most blameworthy nature. In order to obtain a clear grasp of Mme. Guyon's tenets, as well as of the views held by Fénelon, we must begin with a summary of the doctrine of Molinos.[1]

1. Christian perfection consists essentially in an act of contemplation and love, which is continuous, and subsists during the whole of life without requiring to be renewed. This act contains implicitly the acts of all the virtues.

2. In this state of perfection, the soul must cease to reflect on itself, and must annihilate all its powers : this is what is called *quietude*.

3. The soul in this state should go as far as indifference to its eternal salvation.

4. Confession and outward observances become unnecessary.

---

[1] The difference between these three degrees of Quietism are admirably set forth in *l'Analyse de la controverse du Quiétisme* (*cf.* Fénelon, *Œuvres complètes*, iv). The above summary is borrowed from this *Analyse*.

5. In the state of quietude, the soul must remain at rest, and meditate upon no mystery in particular.

6. One must abandon one's free-will to God, and consequently cease to resist temptation. The actions of the bodily and sense part of our nature become foreign to the spiritual part ; and the body may become the instrument of the devil without the soul being responsible.

It can easily be imagined to what immoral and revolting consequences this exaggerated Mysticism might lead.[1] It is also clear that the Church was bound to take alarm at another quite similar doctrine, especially one so closely related to that of Molinos. Of course, in harassing and proscribing that spurious Mysticism which, after Molinos, showed a tendency to be revived within the Church in the doctrine of Mme. Guyon, what was most to be feared, and this was a matter of extreme delicacy, was that a blow might be dealt at true Mysticism, which had been at all times accepted and sanctioned in the Church. It is not surprising that the Prelates hesitated for some time before striking, nor is it to be

[1] *Cf.* Note xxix, p. 271.

wondered at that they were divided; for if
Bossuet was alarmed at the consequences
of Molinos' teaching, which he thought he
discovered in the works of Mme. Guyon,
Fénelon, for his part, might well be anxious
lest the true mystics, identified with, and
compromised by, imprudent and ignorant
disciples, should also incur condemnation.
There were therefore grounds for fearing,
with Fénelon, lest the genuine Saints should
be involved in the censure of Mme. Guyon,
and, with Bossuet, lest the most dangerous
errors should be passed over by her acquittal.
Such then was the grave contest which
arose between the two great Prelates.

At the outset, however, they appeared
to act in agreement. It was to Bossuet
that Mme. Guyon, at Fénelon's instigation,
despatched not only her printed works, but
even all her manuscripts, that he might
examine them. After having taken cog-
nisance of them, and having carefully scru-
tinised them for several months, he deemed
that they were sufficiently harmless to allow
of his admitting the writer of them to Holy
Communion. In the meantime, Bossuet
endeavoured to warn Fénelon against the
dangerous consequences of the new doctrine;

but Fénelon, who was staunch on the principle of pure love, refused to give way, and appealed to the authority of all the great mystics. As for Bossuet, he was as yet so little versed in the literature of Mysticism, that he had recourse to Fénelon himself in order to obtain extracts from the great writers of this school.

Thus, at the start, Bossuet was not ill-disposed towards Mme. Guyon, but was content to advance cautiously on ground with which he was unfamiliar. Fénelon, on his side, was in no way desirous of defending the false mystics, not even Mme. Guyon, whose person he esteemed, and whom he credited with the best of intentions, but without denying that her language was questionable. Hence the resolutions, jointly passed at the Conference of Issy, which recalled :—1st, that every Christian is required to perform separate acts of faith, hope, and love ; 2nd, that an explicit faith in God, the Holy Trinity, and Jesus Christ is enjoined upon every Christian ; 3rd, that he is bound to desire and pray for eternal salvation, remission of sins, and grace ; 4th, that it is not lawful for a

Christian to remain indifferent to his salvation ; 5th, to reflect upon oneself and one's actions is an obligation, even in the case of the most perfect.

The principal duties of positive Christianity were thus restated, and prescribed with firmness, and, as a consequence, the devotional practices which tended to destroy these duties were forbidden. But, at the same time, and it is here that Fénelon's influence is seen, the principles of mystic perfection were expressly retained and authorised. " The prayer of simple presence of God, or of self-surrender and quiet, and the other extraordinary prayers, even passive, approved by Saint Francis de Sales and other mystics, may not be rejected, or held in suspicion, without temerity." It was added, however, in order to prevent untoward consequences, that " it is possible to become a very great saint without these extraordinary prayers," and that " extraordinary ways are rare, and subject to the investigation of the Bishops."

There was a fair appearance that these pronouncements would safeguard both sides. Fénelon had obtained a respite for Mysticism, and Bossuet had secured the prohibition of its excesses. Mme. Guyon appeared to subscribe to everything that was required of her. She declared that she was no theologian, that she renounced any exaggerations which her writings might contain, and that she had no desire to go beyond the teachings of Saint Francis de Sales and the Baroness de Chantal. It seemed, I say, that all was satisfactorily ended. On the contrary, all was starting afresh. Mme. Guyon was about to disappear, or to be relegated to the second plane, and Fénelon was to appear on the first. The battle was now to be waged directly between the two foremost Christian leaders in France. How then had matters come to this pass ?

After the termination of the Conference of Issy, the Commissioners had undertaken to publish, each for his own part, a commentary on the Articles adopted. The two books produced by this controversy are the outcome of this promise : *l'Introduction sur les États d'oraison*, by Bossuet, and *l'Explication des Maximes des Saints*, by Fénelon. Hence all the trouble. They wished to explain, and, as a consequence, they ceased to remain in agreement.

The quarrel began when Fénelon, who

had been requested to signify his approval of Bossuet's work, absolutely refused to do so. It meant a rupture. But why this refusal ? Why should he have been unwilling to subscribe to what, according to Bossuet, was nothing more than a strict commentary on the Articles of Issy ? There was probably a fundamental reason. Fénelon thought that Bossuet went too far in his rejection of Mysticism. But this was not the reason which he alleged. He pleaded his obligations of friendship towards Mme. Guyon, a fact which would not allow of his taking part in any excessive condemnation of her writings. He had been willing to condemn the doctrine itself, but he was not disposed to cast a slur on the character of Mme. Guyon, whose intentions and sentiments he professed to know well, and who had never erred, except in phraseology, a fault which she shared in common with the majority of mystics.

" If I were to give a public token of approval to this interpretation of her system (the interpretation of it given by Bossuet), I should finally persuade the public that it is fair to apply it to her work, and I should thereby acknowledge her to be the most detestable creature on earth. I have seen her much ; I have greatly esteemed her, and have allowed her to be made much of by eminent people who placed reliance upon me. It is not likely that I should have esteemed her, without first going deeply with her into her real opinions. Judging favourably of her person, I commended her doctrine ; at least it must be said that I tolerated an impious system, and that the whole of our intercourse turned only on this pernicious spirituality : this is what would occur to the mind of the reader on finding my approval at the head of M. de Meaux's book, . . . and that is what I am to submit to in the presence of the Church ! I never have defended, and never will defend Mme. Guyon's book, either directly or indirectly ; but I am so intimately acquainted with her intentions by the unlimited confidence which she has placed in me, that I am bound to judge of her writings by her sentiments, and not of her sentiments by her writings. We are constantly reminded that the best mystics have exaggerated. Why should Mme. Guyon be the only one who never exaggerated ? Why must I proclaim by the mouth of M. de Meaux that she breathes a doctrine deserving nothing short of capital punishment ? " [1]

Up to what point was Bossuet right, and how far, on the other hand, was Fénelon not wrong, when the former was so uncompromising in his attack against Mme. Guyon's doctrine, and the latter so generous in his support of it ? We are not required in the interests of our subject to investigate this question, which would need for its settlement a profounder knowledge of theology than we possess. It appears to us, however, after the reading of Mme. Guyon's chief works, extracts of which have been given above, that the errors imputed to her by Bossuet are implicitly, rather than explicitly, contained in her writings. Mme. Guyon, a woman endowed with a lively imagination, who, be it remembered, was no theologian, may very likely, and quite innocently, have fallen into heresy, and that, altogether unintentionally. It is possible that Bossuet himself, had he been unacquainted with Molinos, might have failed to discover more poison in Mme. Guyon than in Saint Teresa or Mme.

[1] Letter to Mme. de Maintenon, August 2, 1696.— *Cf.* Cardinal de Bausset, ii, Pièces justificatives, and *Œuvres* de Fénelon (Lebel edition), ix, p. 89.

de Chantal. Fénelon, for his part, is perhaps too indulgent in not admitting that Mme. Guyon's books contain the germs of the Quietism condemned in Molinos. He was unwilling to confess that he had been misled, and had made a mistake. His complicity in the matter was, in fact, greater than he was disposed to admit, since he had had an intimate knowledge of Mme. Guyon's thoughts for a number of years, having authorised and even introduced them at Saint-Cyr. Matters were doubtless in a dangerous position, and it does not appear that Fénelon made any timely effort to prevent the new Mysticism from degenerating into Quietism. Thus it was both wise and opportune to check the movement. Bossuet's book on the *États d'oraison* put a curb on false Mysticism, but not without having perhaps somewhat compromised the genuine. Fénelon therefore thought himself entitled to draw a fresh distinction between the true and the false. Hence the publication of the *Maximes des Saints* (1697).[1]

Until this time, the disagreement between Bossuet and Fénelon had been entirely of a private character, the absence of Fénelon's

[1] *Cf.* Note xxxix, p. 276.

official approval from his colleague's work being a negative fact, which at most called for surprise and misgiving. But the quarrel soon developed into a doctrinal one, indeed, immediately after the publication of the celebrated work above quoted.

The truth must be stated : whatever ingenuity Fénelon may have possessed, and he revealed this quality in all his works, whatever eloquence and talent he displayed later in his apologetical writings, it must be acknowledged that the question of Quietism hardly ever inspired him prior to the time when his own personality was involved. The *Maximes des Saints* is a mediocre and monotonous work, dull and tiresome to a degree which one would not have expected to find in anything written by Fénelon. Let it not be said that theology is responsible for this. Mme. Guyon's books, however extravagant they may appear, are neither dull nor tiresome ; they are full of fervour, animation, and colour. Bossuet's work on the same subject is also full of vigour and lustre ; the force of its logic gives it movement and warmth. It does not weary us for a single instant. Fénelon's book, on the contrary, is so frigid and spiritless that it repels the reader. Scholastic refinements take the place of the psychological discrimination which one would expect in connection with such a subject. I am not sure whether it was right to condemn Fénelon's book from the theological point of view ; but, from the literary standpoint, it is not to be defended, and it adds nothing to the fame of its author. Its only merit is that it aroused a memorable controversy, in which these two great men vied with each other in eloquence and mutual recriminations (1697).

Such is the venom that lives in the souls of holy men ![1]

Bossuet's first judgment on Fénelon's book runs as follows : " The work is causing a great sensation ; I have not heard the name of a single person who approves of it. Some say that it is badly written ; others that it contains very bold and indefensible ideas ; others, again, that it is written with great delicacy of touch and every conceivable precaution, but that in the main it is not good ; finally, there are those who are of opinion that, at a time when false Mysticism is doing all the harm, nothing should be written about it save by way of condemnation.

[1] *Cf.* Note xl, p. 276.

I pray with all my heart that God may order everything to His glory." [1]

Fénelon decided, of his own accord, in a letter dated April 27, 1697, to lay his book before the Pope. The King, on his side, on July 24 of the same year, also denounced Fénelon's book before the Pope, as " very evil and dangerous, and reproved by the Bishops and a large number of doctors." A few days later, the King requested the Archbishop of Cambrai to retire to his diocese. That day marked the beginning of an. exile which ended only with his life. At the same time Louis XIV refused to allow Fénelon to proceed in person to Rome, in order to vindicate his cause ; this prohibition was scarcely consistent with equity. He was obliged to entrust his cause to a third person, who, fortunately for him, was a most devoted friend, Abbé de Chanterac, whom even a friend of Bossuet calls " a wise, conciliatory, learned, and virtuous man." [2] On the other hand, the interests of the opposite side were committed to a

[1] Letter to Godet-Desmarais, Bishop of Chartres, February 13, 1697. *Cf. Œuvres* de Bossuet (Lebel edition), xl, p. 259.

[2] Manuscripts of Pirot, quoted by Bausset, ii, p. 80.

man of violent and rancorous character, who did his best to envenom the affair, and stimulate the acrimony and bitterness of the Bishop of Meaux : this man was his nephew, Abbé Bossuet.

Then began a series of double dealings which lasted nearly two years : first, in Rome, a secret diplomatic conflict, during which mines and countermines followed alternately on each other, the King pressing for extreme measures and the severest condemnation, the Pope avoiding the issue as far as he was able. The French Ambassador, Cardinal de Bouillon, made every effort to pacify the two parties.

It is easy to understand why Rome should have hesitated between these two eminent prelates. To begin with, Fénelon was perhaps not so absolutely in the wrong as Bossuet and Louis XIV represented him to be. If Fénelon's doctrinal position was too favourable to the false mystics, Bossuet's was perchance too unfavourable to the true. Moreover, Bossuet was not what diplomatists term a *persona grata* in Rome. He was still disliked on account of 1682 and the Four Articles.[1] Between the Pope and the King,

[1] *Cf.* Note xli, p. 277.

BOSSUET AND FÉNELON

Bossuet had too unmistakenly sided with the King to hope to be acceptable to the Roman Curia. It was known, on the other hand, that Fénelon and the Sulpicians were much less Gallican than Bossuet. It was feared that, under the guise of Gallican liberties, servitude towards Rome might be superseded by servitude towards the King. Fénelon therefore enjoyed the secret favour of the Pontifical Court, and Rome seems to have yielded to the persistent and unrelenting pressure of the French Court, rather than to any positive conviction.

While this game was going on in Rome, with all manner of incidental details, into which it is impossible for us to enter here, but which will be found set forth, with evident partiality in favour of Fénelon, in the *Histoire de Fénelon* written by Cardinal de Bausset,—while, I say, the various phases of this diplomatic contest were being enacted, another combat, which relates rather to literary history, was being waged in broad daylight. Bossuet was skilled in these controversies ; Fénelon had not yet tried his hand at them, but the fact of his being threatened in his personal honour and dignity endowed him with a measure of power and fervour, which no one imagined him to possess. He originated a form of eloquence, at once plaintive and lofty, which obtained an immense success ; a form in which humility and dignity were combined, and which was rendered all the more touching because of the harsh and haughty manner of his adversary, a man so accustomed to conquer, that he could not understand how anyone could be found to resist his will.

" When do you wish that we should end this business, my lord ? " writes Fénelon. " If I could declare myself to be in the wrong, and leave the full triumph to you, in order that this scandal might be ended and peace restored to the Church, I would joyfully do so : but, by attempting to reduce me to this course in such a violent manner, you have done precisely what was necessary to deprive me of the means. You impute to me the most abominable impieties *concealed beneath subterfuges disguised as correctives.* Woe to me, were I to keep silence ! My books would be tainted because of such cowardly silence, which would be a tacit admission of impiety. Should the Pope condemn my book, I trust God will give me grace to hold my tongue and obey. But so long as the Holy See allows me to demonstrate my innocence, and so long as I retain a particle of life, I will not cease to call upon Heaven and earth to witness the injustice of your accusations. . . . You rate and magnify everything to suit your requirements, without troubling to make your expressions tally. When you desire to render my retractation easier, you smooth my path ; it is then so pleasant that it loses all its terrors ; you say : '*It is only a short-lived fascination.*' But if anyone makes further inquiry into what you are saying to alarm the Church, they find that this short-lived fascination is '*an unfortunate mystery and a prodigy of seduction.*' Similarly, if your aim is to get me to admit certain writings and visions of Mme. Guyon : '*Is it so great a misfortune,*' you say, '*to have been deceived by a friend?*' But who is this friend ? '*A Priscilla whose Montanus I am.*'[1] . . . We are, you and I, objects of derision to the ungodly, and a source of grief to all truly upright persons. It is not to be wondered at that the average man should act as a man,

[1] This allusion was a gross offence and a species of slander, the relations of Priscilla and Montanus having been carnal as well as spiritual.

but that the ministers of Jesus Christ, the angels of the Church, should present such a spectacle to a profane and faithless world is a thing which calls for tears of blood. Happy indeed should we be if, instead of this war of writings, we had continued our work of catechising in our dioceses, teaching poor village folk both the fear and the love of God ! "[1]

We see how clearly Fénelon, with his intelligence and his sense of worldly affairs, realised that quarrels such as these could only serve the cause of the " esprits forts," the free-thinkers of the time, who were much more numerous than some people imagine. But if this were so, why did he write ? All he was doing, he said, was to defend himself. He was only vindicating his injured honour, it was for Bossuet to hold his peace. The matter was in the hands of the Pope ; all that remained to be done was to await his decision. Fénelon undertook to submit to it. Why was it Bossuet's wish that Fénelon should submit to him, and not to the Church ? Was it necessary to trouble the peace, and to cause a scandal by such violent attacks against an Archbishop and an old friend ?

[1] *Cf.* Note xlii, p. 278.

BOSSUET AND FÉNELON

Bossuet desired to crush heresy single-handed ; he wanted everything to yield to his will. Hence the bitterness and violence of his conduct throughout this affair.

Far from holding his peace, Bossuet, when he realised that the matter was hanging fire in Rome, attempted to deal a decisive blow by the publication of his famous *Relation sur le Quiétisme*. This writing obtained an immense success : " M. de Meaux's book is creating a great stir," wrote Mme. de Maintenon to Cardinal de Noailles (June 20, 1698). "The facts are within the knowledge of everyone ; Mme. Guyon's absurdities are a source of amusement ; the book is short, bright, and well-written ; people are lending it, tearing it from each other, devouring it." And Bossuet's book deserves all this praise, but it must be said that its success was due to indiscretions which might, without exaggeration, be described as breaches of trust. It was from Mme. Guyon's own manuscripts, which she had entrusted to him in all sincerity, in order to prove her innocence before him, manuscripts which clearly did not belong to Bossuet, that the latter extracted the unpublished passages which held up Mme. Guyon to ridicule. As to " the absurdities which are a source of amusement " alluded to by Mme. de Maintenon, how came it that the latter had not noticed them during the years which she had spent in intimacy with Mme. Guyon, and at a time when she had been allowing her to exercise a serious influence at Saint-Cyr ? She had either seen these absurdities, and had passed them over as innocent, or else she had not perceived them ; in the latter case, it may be inquired why she did not offer her testimony, which would have proved an extenuating circumstance in favour of this unhappy woman as well as of Fénelon ?

This time Fénelon appeared to be crushed, and it might have been supposed that he would not recover from the blow. Consternation prevailed in his immediate circle. Moreover, fear of compromising his remaining friends at Court, the Dukes of Beauvillier and Chevreuse, made him keep his counsel : " One must renounce everything," he wrote to his friends, " even the consolation of justifying one's innocence." Fortunately M. de Beauvillier was saved, thanks to the intervention of Cardinal de Noailles with Mme. de Maintenon. Reassured with regard to the fate of his friends, and urged by Abbé de Chanterac, who entreated him to take up his own defence, Fénelon hesitated no longer. He replied in the *Réponse à la Relation de M. de Meaux*. The aspect of things was instantly changed ; the courage of his friends was raised ; the lists were divided ; admiration passed from one side to the other. Those partisans of any contest which may supervene to break the monotony of society life, those friends of beauty and refinement, looked on as at a play, eager to witness the thrusts and counter-thrusts of the two great men who were contending as equals on slippery and dangerous ground.

Fénelon sets out in his *Réponse à la Relation* in the following manner :

" M. de Meaux," he says, " was beginning to feel at a loss concerning the dogmatic side of the issue. In his embarrassment, the story of Mme. Guyon's life seemed to him a spectacle likely to make people forget his numerous miscalculations. This Prelate wishes me to give him a reply on the minutest circumstances relating to the history of Mme. Guyon, just as a criminal at the bar has to answer the judge ; but when I press *him* for a reply on the fundamental points of religion, he complains of my questions. When it is impossible for him to reply on matters of doctrine, he attacks my person ; then he proclaims on the housetop what before he only whispered in the ear ; he resorts to the most odious thing known to men in an organised society : he no longer regards as inviolable the secrecy of private letters, the most sacred thing after the secrecy of the confessional ; he exhibits my letters in Rome ; he has them printed in order to turn to my dishonour the pledges of the boundless trust which I placed in him."

Bossuet, also assuming an apologetical tone, had tried to dissociate his own person from this contest. " Have I," he protested, " the simplest of men, been able alone, and by invisible springs, to cause a commotion throughout the Court, all over Paris, in the entire kingdom, everywhere in Europe, and even in Rome ? " Fixing on this impulse, Fénelon replied : " You will allow me to apply to you what you said against me. What ! Shall I be credited with having assembled, from a corner of my study in Cambrai, and by invisible springs, so many

disinterested and unbiassed persons ? . . .
Have I been able to do for my book—I,
remote, contradicted, and oppressed on all
hands—what M. de Meaux says he was
unable himself to do against this book,
although he was in authority, and in a
position to make himself feared ? "

Finally, Fénelon ended with this haughty
challenge : " If there still remains any writing which M. de Meaux can allege against
me, I entreat him not to make a half-secret
of it, which is worse than an open revelation,
and I implore him to send everything to
Rome. Thank God, I have nothing to fear
from anything that may be communicated
and juridically examined. . . . If he really
thinks me so impious and hypocritical, he
is entitled to make use of all the proofs at
his disposal. As for me, I cannot refrain
from calling to witness Him whose eyes
illumine the darkest recesses, and before
Whom we shall both soon appear. He
knows, for He reads the heart, that I am
devoted only to Him and His Church, and
that I ceaselessly lift up my voice in His
presence, beseeching Him to restore peace,
and make a speedy end of the scandal, to
bring back the pastors to their flocks, and

to vouchsafe to M. de Meaux as many blessings
as he has caused me sorrows." [1]

Fénelon's *Réponse* was a signal revenge
for the success which Bossuet's *Relation* had
obtained. Public favour passed from the
latter to the former. In Rome, as well as
in Paris, a sudden change took place in
people's minds. Bossuet attempted to reply
in his *Remarques sur la Réponse de M. de
Cambrai ;* in answer to this, Fénelon wrote
a *Réponse aux Remarques.* In this last reply,
Fénelon again exhibited the same plaintive
eloquence of which he had previously given
proof ; he returned to Bossuet's indiscreet
comparison of Fénelon and Mme. Guyon
with the heresiarch Montanus and his friend
Priscilla. Bossuet had defended himself by
saying that he had only referred to an *inter-
change of illusions.* Fénelon did not rest
content with this explanation : " This
fanatic," he says, " had caused two of his
women followers to become alienated from
their husbands ; he delivered them over to
a false inspiration which was a veritable
possession of the Evil One. He was himself
as much possessed as these women, and it
was during a transport of demoniacal frenzy

[1] *Cf. Œuvres,* Versailles edition, vi, p. 522.

which had seized him and Maximilla, that they strangled each other. Such is the man, the horror of succeeding ages, to whom you compare your colleague, *a dear and life-long friend, for whom you bear a fatherly affection ;* and you are displeased because he complains of such an odious comparison. No, my lord, I will not complain of it ; I will only be grieved on your behalf."

Alluding to these replies, which seemed to be victorious, at least so far as their mutual transactions were concerned, Bossuet's nephew, who was acting as his agent in Rome, did not scruple to write to his uncle with reference to Fénelon : " He is a wild beast who must be pursued, for the honour of the episcopate and of truth, until he is crushed. Did not Saint Augustine pursue Julian even unto death ? "[1] Can such expressions have been used by a priest writing against a Bishop, and that Bishop, a Fénelon ! Bossuet himself, while not admitting defeat, paid a tribute to his adversary's fine defence : " Let them cease to vaunt his wit and eloquence ; we readily grant that he has defended himself with

[1] Letter from Abbé Bossuet, November 25, 1698. *Cf. Œuvres* de Bossuet, xlii, p. 56.

vigour and obstinacy. Who denies his wit ? He has a frightful amount of it, and his misfortune is to have to defend a cause in which so much wit is required."

The judgment of the Court of Rome came at last. It was not as definite as Louis XIV and Bossuet had desired. Of the ten examiners, five pronounced themselves in favour of a censure and five against. They were thus equally divided, and according to the rules of every tribunal in the world, the accused ought to have reaped the benefit of this evenly balanced vote. The Pope was greatly embarrassed. He tried to divide the blame between the two adversaries : " The Archbishop of Cambrai," he said, " has erred through an excessive love of God ; the Bishop of Meaux has erred through a defective love of his neighbour," but in reality this so-called apportionment was in favour of Fénelon. Such a judgment could not prove acceptable to Louis XIV, who throughout this affair had considered the interests of his sovereign power. He made urgent representations to Rome. The question was again submitted to the examination of the Cardinals, who deliberated for several weeks. They came to the unanimous decision that the book should be censured. But once more the Pope's bias was shown in the choice of the Cardinals, whom he appointed to draw up the censure : they were among those who were particularly favourable to Fénelon ; the Pope himself was on the point of giving a dogmatic decision in place of a direct censure. At this juncture, Louis XIV sent another imperious letter to the Pope. This is the tone in which he addressed him : "His Majesty learns with painful surprise that, after all his earnest entreaties, and the many promises that the harm which is being done in His Kingdom by the Archbishop of Cambrai's book shall forthwith be cut at the root by a formal decision, and when everything appeared to be settled, the partisans of this book propose a new scheme, which would tend to render nugatory so many deliberations. It would be impossible for His Majesty to accept and sanction in His Kingdom anything short of what was promised him, namely, a clear and definite judgment on this book, which is causing such a conflagration in His Kingdom."

Already, without waiting for this letter, the well-nigh insolent haughtiness of which will be perceived, the Pope had yielded, and, in accordance with custom, had declared in a Brief that, *of his own accord (motu proprio), he condemned and reproved the aforesaid book ;* but, while admitting that the work contained certain *rash, scandalous, and offensive* propositions, the Pope refused to qualify them as *heretical,* or even as *bordering on heresy.* [1]

What attitude was Fénelon to adopt ? He had said what he would do time and again during the course of this long controversy, namely, that he would submit ; and in fact he did submit, in terms as dignified as they were simple, in a Charge to the faithful of his diocese :

" We subscribe to this Brief, dearly beloved brethren, both as regards the subject-matter of the book, and the Twenty-three propositions, simply, absolutely, and without qualification or reservation. We condemn them with the same formulas and the same expressions. We exhort you to show a sincere submission and an unexampled obedience. God forbid that we should ever be spoken of, save to recall the fact that a pastor thought fit to be more docile than the least sheep of his flock."

In a letter addressed to the Pope, he

[1] Letter from Abbé Bossuet, March 17, 1699.

repeated his submission in the same terms, adding : " I shall never be ashamed to be reproved by the successor of Saint Peter. I shall never use even the shadow of the slightest equivocation which would tend to evade the decree." Fénelon's adversaries, Phélippeaux[1] and Abbé Bossuet, as well as Bossuet himself, did not appear to be satisfied with this submission, and the latter saw in it " a considerable amount of ambiguity and ostentation." Instead of admitting his errors, they accused him of having referred only to his humiliation and docility. But soon universal approval of Fénelon's attitude forced them to change their tone : " In spite of the defects in M. de Cambrai's Charge, I think one ought to be satisfied with it, because, after all, it contains everything that is essential, and obedience is magnificently displayed."

One wonders whether Fénelon's submission was as real inwardly as outwardly, whether a man can really divest himself of his thoughts and beliefs, in other words, of what appears to him to be evident. For example, could Fénelon, under such circumstances, cease to believe that all the great

[1] *Cf.* Note xliii, p. 278.

mystics had spoken practically in the same
terms as he had ; could he declare them to
be wrong, and thus, as it were, suppress all
Mysticism in the Church, or else proclaim
that they were in the right, without con-
tradicting in his inmost heart his apparent
retractation ? Fénelon himself has replied to
this objection :[1] doubtless, all he had done
was to reproduce what he had found in all
the works on higher Mysticism ; but it is
one thing to make use of a few imprudent
expressions, inadvertently employed in works
of piety, the authors of which were not
theologians, and who, carried away by
their feelings, were not able to measure and
weigh all their words ; it is quite another
thing for an Archbishop to write a dogmatic work, such as the *Maximes des Saints*,
dealing with a controverted subject, and
claiming to make an exact apportionment
between truth and error. If Rome wished
to correct all the theological inaccuracies
contained in the most pious works, she
would spend all her time in condemna-
tions, for piety is not theology. She inter-
venes only when the expressions above
alluded to assume a doctrinal significance,

[1] Ramsay, *Vie de Fénelon*, pp. 92, 95.

and become a species of dogma. Fénelon could therefore admit, without lapsing from the truth, that he had perchance erred in taking too literally certain statements which were mere verbal exaggerations on the part of the mystics.

This was so reasonable a distinction, that Fénelon had, so to speak, drawn it himself before his condemnation. In the controversy which had followed the publication of his *Maximes*, Fénelon had amended, softened, qualified, and explained, in a more orthodox sense, the passages for which he was reproached, and which were open to questionable interpretations, and he had done this with so much care that the Court of Rome, after having condemned the *Maximes*, did not censure the apologetical writings which had followed the *Maximes ;* and consequently, in the controversy between Bossuet and Fénelon, Rome neither approved nor blamed either of the protagonists. Despite Bossuet's endeavours to obtain the condemnation of the apologetical writings,[1] the latter remained authorised, and they express one side of the truth, the other side of which was grasped by Bossuet with

[1] *Cf.* Note xliv, p. 278.

accuracy and firmness, although with a certain narrowness.

In his fine *Histoire de la Littérature française*, D. Nisard seems to lay all the blame on Fénelon, and to justify Bossuet entirely. According to him, Bossuet represents what this eminent critic appreciates above all else : common sense and the love of order. Fénelon, on the contrary, typifies nothing but individualism and a wildly imaginative mind. This is, perhaps, too easy a solution of a very difficult problem. Even from the theological point of view, we have seen that the question was not so simple, since it had required two years to examine, the first judges had been equally divided, and the Pope had long hesitated before inflicting a censure ; moreover, in order to secure a final settlement, the direct intervention of Louis XIV, who was no theologian, had been needed ; finally, the Pope had absolutely refused to make use of the term *heresy*. But let us set theology aside, and examine the matter in itself, and from the philosophical point of view. What did the discussion turn upon ? Wherein lay the chief point of the difficulty ? No one imputed to Fénelon the gross errors of Molinos, and, in particular, the revolting doctrine that, in the state of holiness, such a separation between soul and body takes place, that everything which happens in the body is foreign to the soul, and that it can commit the most criminal acts without the soul being responsible. It was not even possible to impute to Fénelon the modified Quietism of Mme. Guyon, who rejected the views of Molinos concerning the irresponsibility of the soul for the disorderly actions of the body,[1] but whose teaching tended to do away with all forms of practical piety, such as vocal prayers, a clear vision of the mysteries, separate acts of love, faith, and hope, and the careful examination of the self. Fénelon repudiated all these exaggerations which he had condemned with his colleagues at the Conferences of Issy.[2] For him the question centred round the love of God. And here, it seems to us, neither of the adversaries was absolutely right, nor absolutely wrong. Of course, from the practical point of view, and from the standpoint of average actual facts, Bossuet was justified in refusing to weaken man's desire for salvation,

[1] *Cf.* p. 71, *supra*, and Note xxix, p. 271.

[2] *Cf.* Bausset, ii, p. 249.

which is the strongest link binding man to religion. Psychologically, too, Bossuet was right in asserting that it is chimerical to wish to destroy in man all forms of self-love and of desire for happiness. He therefore fancied he recognised in Fénelon the Quietist doctrine of indifference to salvation, a dangerous doctrine, which would deprive man of all personal energy and of all striving after virtue. As a matter of fact, Fénelon had made the mistake of taking in too literal a sense the mystic principle of indifference to salvation, and he had been obliged to admit, in his apologetical explanations, that the act of hope and confidence in God should never be absent from the Christian life ; but was he not also right, if not from the point of view of common practice, at least from that of Christian perfection, in maintaining that, although the hope of salvation is implicitly contained in the love of God, it ought not to be the motive of that love ; that we must not love God for the sake of our own salvation, or for the benefits, even spiritual, which we may reap thereby, but that we must believe in salvation for the sole reason that we love God ?

Fénelon was thus not wholly chimerical in this controversy. He stood for the interests of the highest and purest aspect of the soul's activities, if only in the name of an ideal, clearly not to be realised by us here, but towards which we must tend as far as we are able. The doctrine of pure love represents an essential point of view, both in theology and in ethics. This doctrine may doubtless be exaggerated—and it is possible that Fénelon carried it to extremes, since his *Maximes* were condemned,—but it is not harmful in itself, seeing that the vindications he gave of it later, in his controversy with Bossuet, were not censured.[1]

To sum up. In this question as in all others, Fénelon shows himself submissive to the principles of tradition, albeit with a tendency towards independence and individuality. He is never content with the commonplace. He always aims at something different from the ordinary. He has the instincts not of revolt, but of liberty. He does not like to think exactly what other people are thinking, and he always seeks to get to the bottom of

[1] *Cf.* Note xlv, p. 280.

everything. For the preservation of a Church, a Bossuet is more necessary than a Fénelon ; but without Fénelon the Church would have lacked one of her most beautiful ornaments.

CHAPTER VI

FÉNELON AS SPIRITUAL DIRECTOR

FÉNELON possessed all the qualities which are needed to make an accomplished spiritual director. Powers of persuasion, gentleness, consideration for the feelings of others, moral elevation, insinuation—such were the instruments of action he employed in dealing with devout souls. Moreover, he knew the world and had a lofty outlook on life. Doubtless it might be feared that his counsels contained rather too great an element of spirituality ; indeed, the memory of his bold mystical speculations had cast somewhat of a shadow over this part of his writings. Accordingly, when his nephew, the Marquis de Fénelon, wished to publish his *Lettres spiri-tuelles* (1719), he encountered grave obstacles, and even positive obstruction, on the part of certain Prelates. But theory is one thing, and practice another. A position which may cause some scruples, when considered from the point of view of dogma, may be more or less sanctioned in the guidance of devout souls, where it is impossible to weigh every word. The letters of Saint Francis de Sales are full of mystical sentiments and expressions, which differ but slightly from those of Fénelon. Bossuet himself, in his spiritual letters to certain Sisters, also makes free use of very bold expressions, which he would perhaps have condemned in a dogmatic form, and from Fénelon's pen. We will, however, set aside those parts in the *Lettres spirituelles* which savour of higher Mysticism, and which pertain to theology rather than to literature ; instead, we will seek everything that relates to the life of this world. Many excellent counsels in this connection are to be found in the *Instructions, ou Avis sur différents points de la morale et de la perfection chrétienne.*[1] It is thought that much of this advice was addressed to Mme. de Maintenon. Nothing is more likely, if we bear in mind how appropriate these counsels were to the particular position of this illustrious lady. The problem in the case of Mme. de Maintenon, who was at once in the highest worldly station, and in the loftiest state of religious devotion, was how to satisfy the requirements of this

[1] *Cf. Œuvres,* xviii, p. 193. These Instructions do not form part of the *Lettres spirituelles,* although they are really spiritual epistles.

twofold position. Fénelon's advice is prompted by the most discriminating tact, and the keenest feeling for the exigencies of life. What attitude should she adopt towards the pleasures and dissipations of the Court ? She must bear with them, and join only in those that are necessary : " You must not worry about the amusements in which you cannot avoid taking part. . . . Some people want us to fret about everything. . . . I cannot bring myself to agree with such excessive strictness. . . . When God places people in certain high stations where they are compelled to share in every function, they have only to remain in peace without worrying continually about the secret motives, which may imperceptibly steal into the heart. . . . God is not satisfied with the utterances of the lips, or the postures of the body, or with outward ceremonies ; what He requires is a will which desires nothing and refuses nothing, but accepts wholeheartedly whatever He ordains. . . . You tell me you would prefer to be busied with more serious and substantial matters. But God does not desire a better lot for you."

The chains of a Court are, without question,

golden chains, and they do not chafe less than iron chains ; yet, by being resigned to them, one may change them into sources of happiness and freedom : " We wish to be free in order to think of God ; but it is far easier to attain union with Him by the mortification of the will, than by the consolation obtained through sweet and loving meditation on His favours. We wish to be more our own masters, in order to give ourselves more completely to God ; but nothing is less calculated to bring us to God, than the endeavour to remain still our own masters. The *self* of the old man to which we strive to revert, in order to be united with God, is infinitely further removed from Him, than the most worthless bauble ; for this self contains a subtle poison which is not to be found in the amusements of childhood."

Mme. de Maintenon was fond of retiring to Saint-Cyr[1] in order to rest from Court life. Fénelon approves and encourages these retreats ; but he will not have her idle : " When you are at Saint-Cyr, you must rest your body, unburden your mind, and concentrate it upon God. You are so tied

[1] *Cf.* Note xxvi, p. 268.

down, worried, and fatigued at Versailles, that you require to find at Saint-Cyr a haven of solitude, at once leisurely, and fortifying to the soul. Yet I would not have you fail to attend to the urgent requirements of the establishment." There must be no excessive mortifications : " I would rather that you suffered less and loved more. Nothing is more erroneous and unworthy than the desire to choose always, and in all things, what is vexatious. I beseech you to remain in peace in this straight and simple line of conduct. Be free, cheerful, natural, like a child, only a bold child, who fears nothing, says everything artlessly, and who, although carried in arms, possesses a liberty and fearlessness denied to grown-up people." We must keep our eyes open to the unpleasant things of life, but not to the point of being discouraged by them : " We must let temptation rage around us, as a traveller, overtaken by a mighty wind, wraps himself round with his cloak, and pursues his way in spite of the bad weather. . . . When one has satisfied a discreet confessor, one has only to cast all one's sins into the unfathomable depths of the divine mercy." We must not long for great and unattainable virtues and sacrifices, but we must remain content with the small ones which are within our reach : " Saint Francis de Sales says that high virtues and little loyalties are like sugar and salt. Sugar has a more excellent savour, but it is not for frequent use ; salt, on the other hand, enters into every item of food."

Fénelon shows himself very severe against what he terms " pharisaic righteousness," which is entirely concerned with external things : " They fast and give alms, but without love of God, humility, or sacrifice of self. They are content, provided they have before them a certain number of works regularly performed : such people are Pharisees. Another defect of pharisaic righteousness is that a man comes to lean upon it as upon his own strength. He takes a great delight in considering his own uprightness, in being conscious of his own powers, and in mirroring himself in his virtue, as a vain woman does in her looking-glass."

Mme. de Maintenon had requested Fénelon to acquaint her with her faults. This was an exceedingly delicate task, as well as a great responsibility, even for a priest to undertake. Nothing could be at once more ingenious, or noble, than the letter which Fénelon wrote on this subject.[1] He passed everything off by tracing all her faults to her qualities. He seems to have given a true delineation of her character, for it is practically the conception we form of Mme. de Maintenon.

"You are frank and unaffected," he tells her ; " you behave very well towards those whom you like ; but when you are severe, you carry your severity too far." He reveals her predominating characteristic : love of glory and worldly esteem ; he was only telling her what she often said to herself : " You are naturally very vain-glorious, you long for the good opinion of people of rank, you covet the pleasure of upholding your prosperity with moderation, and of appearing above your station by the qualities of your heart. The *self* is an idol which you have not yet broken down." He hints tactfully at what was being said about her : " It is said, and according to all appearances with some degree of truth, that you are cold and stern, and that, being severe with yourself, you are harsh towards others. If this is a true portrait of you, this fault

[1] *Cf. Correspondance,* v, p. 466.

will only be removed by a prolonged and thorough study of yourself."

Fénelon was led to touch on her conduct with the King, and her influence over public affairs. This meant broaching a delicate subject, upon which he was perhaps not required to offer advice; but he alluded. to it so discreetly, that his hints were doubtless not resented. It was an inveterate habit with Mme. de Maintenon to assert that she was unskilled in state affairs; but she did not take offence when she was told that possibly she was more competent than she imagined : " You are too diffident as regards your powers; you are too fearful of entering into discussions which are repugnant to your fondness for a quiet and contemplative life." Yet he is very far from urging her to interfere indiscriminately in the King's concerns : " To speak with overmuch warmth and peevishness, to be too insistent, to erect underground batteries, to formulate plans of worldly wisdom—all this is to attempt to do good by wrong means."

He goes on to speak to her of the King : " Your endeavours to interest and instruct him, to enlarge his heart, to guard him from certain snares, to give him visions of peace, above all to move him to improve the lot of the people, and to urge upon him moderation, equity, distrust of harsh and violent counsels, abhorrence of acts of arbitrary authority, . . . such is the occupation which I place above every other in your case."

He penetrates very far into the realms of Mysticism, and even borders on a rather fanatical form of asceticism, when he preconises the abandonment of all relish for friendship and goodness of heart. He himself experienced only too well the success which his counsels obtained, for neither friendship nor kindness followed him in his fall and exile. But he did not think of these consequences when he wrote : " True goodness of heart consists in fidelity to God. All generosity, all natural affection, is only self-love of a more subtle, delusive, gratifying, delightful, and diabolical quality. One must wholly die to all friendship." This is going very far indeed, for after having sacrificed human friendships, shall we be quite sure of putting genuine love of God in their place ?

With regard to family life, he lays down two rules : " Not to refuse to speak in

FÉNELON

favour of one's kinsmen, when it is reasonable to do so, and not to be angry when one's recommendation meets with no success." Finally, war against the self is always Fénelon's last word : "Uncompromising renouncement of this wretched *self*,—that is the true crucifying of the flesh." [1]

Fénelon's most lengthy spiritual correspondence is the one he exchanged with Countess de Montberon. It is principally concerned with one of the maladies most frequently met with in religious devotion, and one of the best known to spiritual directors : the malady of scruples. There are many books on the subject. [2] Fénelon wages a perpetual warfare against this infirmity, as well as against the spirit of excessive unrest and mental agitation in the service of God (Letters 244–247). He enjoins simple and childlike surrender to Providence (Letters 249–252). He combats religious scruples (254) ; he inquires into their origin, and into the ways of curing them (251). He shows the wrongfulness of exaggerated scrupulosity (257).

It must be admitted that there was a

[1] *Cf.* Note xlvi, p. 280.
[2] *Cf.* Note xlvii, p. 280.

great deal of discouragement in the manner in which Fénelon fought against these scruples. The spiritual adviser himself stood in need of an adviser : " As for me," he wrote, " I am in a state of arid, gloomy, and languishing peace ; without troubles, without pleasures, and with no thought of having any ; my present condition is dull and often difficult, yet with a something that carries and alleviates each cross, and leaves me contented, but spiritless. . . . The world appears to me like a poor comedy which will end in a few hours. I despise myself even more than the world ; I suppose the worst in every case, and it is at the lowest depths of this black outlook that I find peace." Is this, O Fénelon, the language of a worthy spiritual director ? Is it for you to. teach a weak and sensitive soul distaste for all earthly things, weariness of life, and peace in the last degree of indifference ? If that is Quietism, it is an unwholesome Quietism, recalling the Nirvana of Buddhism. Are there not in life positive affections and duties, which summon, strengthen, rejoice, and compel us ? And is it not a morbid refinement of the imagination to discover everywhere naught but inanity and nothingness ? Such sentiments may be all very well for the cloister, and even there I should consider them dangerous, but they are of no practical value for life in the world. A little Mysticism is a good thing, but too much Mysticism is pernicious, and only conduces to the breaking of all the springs of action. Who will attain the energy necessary for activity, after such a whole-sale renunciation ? Is not this so-called surrender to God rather a yielding to one-self, and would it not be the same if one believed in nothing whatever ?

This extreme languor and barrenness of soul was precisely the moral sickness from which Fénelon's penitent suffered. He only succeeded in increasing her malady. And yet no one perceived more clearly than he, the worthlessness of these false scruples to which she was a prey. He had a clear per-ception of this, and he told her the truth, but to no purpose. Fresh starts had con-stantly to be made : " You are in a state of agitation, your soul is dried up ; you are wandering away from God . . . in your troubled search after all these trifles which your imagination magnifies. Let me put them in the worst light, and suppose them to be real sins; even then they can be nothing more than venial sins which call for self-abasement. . . . Turn your over-scrupulous sensitiveness against your moral qualms (257). True love of God dispels all scruples (258)."

The rest of the correspondence continues in the same tone, and on the same subject. He asks her to go to confession without fear or scruple (262); to overcome her scruples by guarding against her imagination (264); to avoid arguments and refined forms of introspection (267) : submissiveness, simple blind obedience, such is the remedy for over-scrupulousness (274–276). In a word, it deals throughout exclusively with scruples ; and yet the correspondence lasts ten years. It is clear that Fénelon obtained no good results, seeing that, to the very end, he was always starting anew. The malady of scruples is a kind of spiritual hypochondria, over which religious direction seems to have no more influence than ordinary medicine over physical hypochondria.

Of all Fénelon's labours which relate to spiritual direction, the most remarkable was the conversion of Andrew Ramsay (le Chevalier de R.). It deserves to detain us for a few moments.

FÉNELON

Ramsay[1] was a Scotch nobleman, attached to the cause of the Stuarts, who had made France his country of adoption, and had become so thoroughly naturalised that he wrote all his works in French, in a noble, elegant, and generally pure style. He belonged to the little Court of Saint-Germain in which the Pretender vegetated, and he died there in 1743. His chief title to fame, it must be confessed, resides in the fact that he was the friend, disciple, and convert of Fénelon.

At the beginning of the eighteenth century, as is well known, the mental frame of mind most generally prevalent, both in London and Paris, was a bold and scoffing scepticism, which was usually rather superficial, sometimes stopping short of the limits of natural religion, but more often advancing beyond them, and above all extremely hostile to Christianity. Voltaire was not the inventor of this form of scepticism : he had himself met with, and imbibed it, first in Paris, in the society of the Temple, then in London, in the company of the wits, Collins, Toland, and Bolingbroke ; but his genius appropriated it, and he diffused it over his century and gave ˄his name to it.

[1] *Cf.* Note xlviii, p. 280.

FÉNELON AS SPIRITUAL DIRECTOR

In the midst of this irreligion,—*libertinage*, as it was then called,—is it not a most interesting spectacle to see a sceptic of quite another cast, one totally unlike the others of the period, a restless and tormented sceptic, thirsting for truth, and, in Pascal's notable words, seeking it with groanings ? Such an one was the Chevalier de Ramsay. Born in Scotland, that austere country upon which the religion of Calvin and Knox has left so profound a mark, his soul was uninfluenced by the superficial scepticism of the courts and towns ; and yet the contradictions of the sects, their fanaticism and superstition, revolted his mind, and filled him with the bitterest despair. At one time, he tells us, he was on the point of plunging into atheism, but the outlook filled him with horror. In deism, he found a more satisfactory answer to the claims of his reason ; but he thought it incomplete, vague, cold, and lacking in authority. He examined all the religions in his search after truth ; he went as far as Holland to consult Pastor Poiret,[1] the celebrated mystic, who gave him but scant satisfaction ; finally, his good fortune took him to Cambrai, and

[1] *Cf.* Note xlix, p. 281.

it was there that his soul, led captive, and, as it were, enchanted, by the exquisite words of the most spiritual and kindly of Christian priests, abdicated into the hands of Catholic authority. He has left us an account of his conversations with the noble Archbishop ; this narrative, if I may make so bold a comparison, is a kind of inverted profession of faith of the Savoyard Vicar.[1] Ramsay, anticipating Rousseau, pours out his secret thoughts with the utmost candour. Fénelon penetrates, consoles, caresses, and, so to speak, envelops his soul, leaving it only prostrated. Who could resist such words, which probably no other would have dared to utter at that time : " He who has not experienced all the mental conflicts through which you are passing in your search after truth, does not realise its value. Open your heart to me. Do not fear to shock me ; I see your wound ; although it is deep, it is not past healing, since you lay it open before me." In speaking thus, is not this noble-minded priest foreseeing, and unwittingly favouring, modern doubt, that sincere, deep-seated, anxious, yet fear-less doubt, which suffers from being unable

[1] *Cf.* Note 1, p. 281.

to believe, but which delights and takes a pride in its suffering ? As for Ramsay, he surrendered, and followed Fénelon, whose principles he approved and adopted, and whose writings he imitated. He evinced his gratitude by publishing a very interesting *Vie de Fénelon*, which contains details only to be found there, and in particular the words we have just quoted.

All the spiritual letters do not deal exclusively with the subtleties and perplexities of the inner life. They were addressed to all kinds of people, and treat of many different subjects. Fénelon advises an Archbishop (Colbert, Archbishop of Rouen) not to allow himself to be dragged into luxurious building : "You have seen," he writes to him, "only too many domestic examples of the imperceptible manner in which people get entangled in this sort of enterprise. The temptation begins by creeping in stealthily ; it wears a modest aspect at first, for fear of offending, but later it becomes tyrannical. One scheme leads on to another ; you notice that one part of the work is brought into dishonour by another : every fresh improvement strikes you as mediocre, the whole becomes superfluous and extravagant.

Building, like gambling, is a passion; a house becomes a mistress. Who will cure the mania for building?"

To a military man, who asks his advice concerning levies in field time, he offers very practical suggestions: "1st, to forage like the rest of the army: it would create a scandal to appear to condemn the only method by which the King wishes or, indeed, is able, to make provision for his troops; 2nd, as for fruit trees, I cannot permit them to be used as fuel; 3rd, to be content with cutting off the branches of trees which do not yield fruit; 4th, to avoid taking from the owner anything which the financial arrangements of the camp enable you to purchase. When the difficulty of purchasing becomes insurmountable, taking may be considered an absolute necessity; it is one of the inevitable evils which war carries in its train."

To a young man who moved in Court circles, he gives counsels of meditation and devotion, which were not inconsistent with the obligations of his rank. He points out two pitfalls: indolence and amusements. He warns him against excessive austerity: "It is to be feared that your religious

152

sentiments may lead you little by little into a particular mode of life which, on the whole, will have nothing solid about it. You will reckon it a great thing to keep clear of the company of mad-brained youths, and you will fail to perceive that religion is only your pretext to shun them. All this will immerse you in more serious and sober habits of life, but beware lest this seriousness become as vacuous as their gay folly." Instead of his supercilious and unsociable aloofness, he advises him to present a civil countenance to everyone in all the places where people congregate, at Court in the King's presence, as well as in the army among the generals. " You must try and acquire a certain degree of politeness. . . . There must be no vaunting airs, no affectation. When it becomes known that you are labouring to be proficient in everything that pertains to history and warfare, no one will dare upbraid you on the score of devotion."

It is clear that Fénelon was able, when he so wished, to harmonise spiritual mindedness with a just appreciation of the requirements of life and society. He did not think that devotion should take the place of everything else ; he desired the pious man to be a gentleman at the same time, according to the world's estimate. In his eyes, perfection was not incompatible with wisdom, and he was unwilling to allow piety to degenerate into eccentricity. Simplicity was his rule in all things; and this simplicity was as far removed from a rigid and prideful spiritual direction, as from worldly vanity and profane ambition.

CHAPTER VII

" TÉLÉMAQUE "

AT the time of its publication, in the year 1699, *Télémaque* [1] obtained a prodigious success, of the kind which attaches to a satire or a political pamphlet, for this was the significance which was first given to it on all sides. People saw in it a severe and malevolent criticism of the Court and government of Louis XIV. Such a criticism fell in with the feelings of bitterness and jealousy engendered in Europe by Louis XIV, as well as with the hatred felt by the Protestant refugees, and with the smouldering opposition which prevailed throughout France. *Télémaque* was translated into every language of Europe, and even to-day, in many countries, it is still in *Télémaque* people learn French.

Its success as a work of opposition was destined to pass with the lapse of time. *Télémaque* then became the reading book of children, the first novel put into the hands of youth. We have all been charmed by

[1] *Cf.* Note li, p. 281.

the work at one time or another ; but hardly anyone to-day reads it again in maturer years. We have read too many novels, we are too surfeited with romantic adventures and the portrayal of the passions, for *Télémaque* to rouse a lively interest in us now-a-days. It must be read from a literary point of view ; it will then be found to contain great beauties.

Télémaque is an imitation of Homer's *Odyssey*. Instead of the voyages of Ulysses and his peregrinations across the seas in order to return to Ithaca, and be reunited to his faithful Penelope, Fénelon narrates the story of the adventures of Telemachus in search of his father Ulysses. This was a favourable scheme in which to work in an infinite number of reminiscences of the great epics of antiquity : the *Iliad*, the *Odyssey*, and the *Aeneid*. Allusions to the Trojan war, and quotations from Virgil and Homer, would be met with at every turn. It was also a framework for adventures which were bound to charm and amuse the minds, still so little sophisticated, of the readers of the time.

Not only is the subject of *Télémaque* borrowed from antiquity, the work itself is also full of classical reminiscences and imitations. The journeys of Telemachus recall the wanderings of Ulysses in the *Odyssey*. The island of Calypso suggests that of Circe. But the intoxicating beverages, by which Circe transforms the companions of Ulysses into brutes, are here replaced by the more delusive, and not less dangerous, infatuations of love. Telemachus escapes from the temptations of Calypso just as Ulysses does from those of Circe. It is likewise from the *Odyssey* that Fénelon borrows the ingenious artifice by which Minerva is concealed behind the features of Mentor. The speech of Telemachus to the goddess reminds us of the discourse of Aeneas before Venus on his landing in Africa, and of that of Aeneas before Dido, when he appears in the presence of the Queen ; the two last discourses likewise recall to our minds similar speeches in the *Odyssey*. The narrative of the storm, in the First Book, is an imitation of the one in the *Aeneid*. It is also from the *Aeneid* that Fénelon borrows the episode of Pygmalion, which he relates at much greater length. The dream of Telemachus is an imitation of the dreams in ancient literature, and in

particular of that of Aeneas (Book II of the
Aeneid). The episode of Idomeneus is a
reminiscence of the *Odyssey* and the *Aeneid*
(Book III). The battles and games of the
First Book of *Télémaque* remind us of those
related in the *Aeneid* (Book V). The riddles
also are an echo of Greek antiquity, when
people were passionately fond of this kind
of witticism. Calypso's complaints against
the coldness of the young hero put us in
mind of the lamentations of Dido and of
Ariadne when similarly deserted. The description of Bætica is reminiscent of the
accounts of the golden age, given by Hesiod
and Virgil. The prayers of Venus, beseeching Jupiter to sacrifice Telemachus, recall
those of Juno entreating Jupiter against
the Trojans. The foundation of the city
of Salentum reminds us of the foundation
of Carthage in the *Aeneid* (Book I). The
republic of Salentum is an imitation of
Plato's *Republic*, and a reminiscence of the
old idealised constitutions of Crete and
Lacedæmon. The charming description of
agricultural life is an echo of the well-known
passage in the *Georgics : O fortunatos !* The
maxims relating to education take us back
to Xenophon's *Cyropædia*. The shield of

Telemachus is an imitation of Achilles' shield in Homer, and of that of Aeneas in the *Aeneid*. We have already called attention to the fact that entire Books are imitations and translations. The Book on Philoctetes is a translation from Sophocles. The description of the Elysian Fields is a modified imitation of the *Aeneid* (Book VI). There are even closer imitations. The entrance to Hell is taken from Virgil. The whole of the description of Tartarus is almost entirely translated. The Elysian Fields are also an imitation, but one which is perhaps superior to the model. Mention must also be made of the funeral of Hippias, a ceremony often described by the Ancients, as, for example, the funeral of Patroclus and Hector. We are pointing out only those portions of the work which are of a certain length ; but at every step we recognise the style, the spirit, and the very expressions of Virgil and Homer. Homeric epithets are frequent. The songs of Apollo reproduce a thousand similar songs : " He celebrated the flowers which improve the graces of spring . . ." The taming of the wild beasts reminds us of Orpheus in Horace. We find at every turn comparisons taken from the simplest and most familiar objects : the death of a young man compared to a flower cut down with the scythe : "The goddess towered above her companions, as a great oak in the forest towers above all the neighbouring trees." All this is a souvenir of antiquity.

In a word, Fénelon borrowed from the Ancients his subject, characters, and principal episodes; numerous details, such as dreams, songs, storms, battles, games, and contests; finally his most usual descriptions and comparisons. Let us now dwell on a few of the most beautiful or brilliant episodes.

Behold Apollo tending the flocks of King Admetus, and charming the shepherds with his delightful songs : "He sang of the flowers which crown the spring, the fragrance which she diffuses, and the verdure that rises under her feet. Then he sang of the sweet evenings of summer, her zephyrs that refresh mankind, and her dews that allay the thirst of the earth. . . . He described the gloomy forests with which the mountains are overshadowed, and the hollow valleys with their meandering rivers, which flow sportively through luxuriant meadows.

And thus he taught the shepherds the happiness that is to be found in a rural life."

By the side of these graceful pictures, there are others which are full of vigour and fire : " One day a hungry lion chanced to break in among my flock ; I advanced boldly towards him, although I had nothing in my hand but my sheep-hook. The lion erected his mane, showed me his teeth, and extended his claws ; he opened his dry and inflamed mouth, and his eyes had a red and fiery appearance ; with his long tail he beat his flanks. I threw him to the ground ; three times I brought him low ; three times he rose against me, roaring so loudly that the utmost recesses of the forest echoed ; at last, I grasped him till he was strangled." Doubtless it is not a common sight to see a man strangle a lion ; but we are in the realm of poetry, still close to the heroic ages, and not far from the exploits of Hercules.

The narratives are no less brilliant than the descriptions. The scene of the sacrifice of Idomeneus is profoundly tragical, and worthy of a painter. As is well known, Idomeneus, like Theseus in *Phædra*, has made an inconsiderate vow. He has promised Neptune, in order that the latter may save him during a shipwreck, to offer up to him the first human being that shall meet his gaze. It is his own son upon whom his eyes first rest : " He beholds his son ; he starts back filled with horror. . . . Meanwhile his son throws his arms round his neck : ' O my father ! what is the cause of this sorrow ? What have I done ? You turn your eyes from me as if you dreaded to behold me.' " Idomeneus admits his vow, and makes an effort to plunge his sword into his own bosom. Sophronymus, a hoary prophet, endeavours to dissuade him from executing so rash a vow : " Your promise was unadvised ; the gods are not to be honoured by cruelty." Idomeneus listened to this address with bowed head, and made no reply ; his eyes sparkled with fury. His visage became ghastly, his colour changed every moment. Meanwhile his son said : " Here am I, my father ; your son is ready to die in order to appease the god ; do not bring down his anger upon your head." These loving and resigned words recall those of Iphigenia in Racine's tragedy. The breath of Christianity has passed over them, and the sacrifice of Idomeneus reminds us of Abraham's sacrifice.

All the examples we have cited above suffice to show how poetical is *Télémaque*, although it is written in prose. But the work is not only a poetical romance, it is also, in the words of Voltaire,[1] *un roman moral*, an educational novel. It touches not only on ethics, but on politics and religion. These three subjects are inseparably linked together in the book. Being designed for a Prince, the ethical teaching nearly always bears upon the art of reigning. Moreover, seeing it is a goddess who speaks by the mouth of Mentor, she is always reminding her hearers of the gods, and ethics and religion are blended in her speeches. Mentor has been reproached, no doubt rightly, for his sermonising propensities : a goddess ought to speak in a less monotonous fashion, nor ought she to utter so many commonplaces. Such moralising might easily impress youth in a manner contrary to the one desired. This ethical bias is, however, rendered more interesting, even as in Fénelon's own day it was invested with a more pointed significance, from the fact that the critical acumen

[1] *Cf.* Note lii, p. 282.

of readers detected in it a covert opposition to, and an indirect satire of, Louis XIV, his morals, and mode of government. These commonplaces assume a singular forcefulness, when they are considered in the light of their time and place-setting. Despite all Fénelon's denials, it is hardly possible to doubt that his chief aim was to criticise, and that his ulterior design was to prepare a different conception of government in the mind of the future sovereign, who was destined to succeed Louis XIV. This critical spirit predominates throughout, together with a certain amount of bitterness. With the exception of Sesostris, the author usually introduces us to bad Kings (Bocchoris, Pygmalion, Idomeneus before his reformation, Adrastus). He places the majority of the Kings in Hell, leaving very few in the Elysian Fields. All the censures addressed to Kings are peculiarly applicable to Louis XIV : conquests, wars, pomp and luxury, flatterers, all powerful and prevaricating ministers (Louvois under the garb of Protesilaus), and absolutism. He draws a picture of a people oppressed and despoiled by its masters, and contrasts it with an ideal and utopian vision of a perfectly happy people (Bætica and Salentum).

Independently of this somewhat chimerical, and platonic, critical spirit, inspired by arm-chair politics, and preconising peace, moderation, simplicity of manners, the need of rules, and the limitation of taxes, *Télémaque*, in spite of its pagan setting, is the outcome of another inspiration, which raises its ethical standpoint above that of the pagan world, namely, the inspiration of Christianity. We may safely assert that it is this inspiration that animates Fénelon when he constantly places peace above war ; for this is a doctrine that has very little in common with the genius of antiquity, which set military glory above everything else. It is this inspiration which causes him to proclaim the brotherhood of all peoples (Book XII), a conception peculiar to Christianity ; it is the same inspiration which leads him to make Mentor tell Telemachus that his virtue does not proceed from himself, but from a power outside himself, which has been " given him,"—an obvious allusion to the doctrine of grace (Book XII). It is of the Christian scriptures that Fénelon is thinking, when he speaks of " that simple, infinite, immutable light, which gives itself to everything without being divided, that sovereign truth which illumines every mind, just as the sun sheds light on the body" (Book X) : is not this the light "which lighteth every man that cometh into the world," of which St. John speaks ? The descriptions of Hell and the Elysian Fields are also inspired by the Christian spirit. It is Christianity which, in the place of the material punishments of classical mythology, suggests to him that crime is its own chastisement (Book XVIII). Finally, it is Christianity that prompts him to draw that masterly picture of the Elysian Fields, where the merely material happiness of the pagan world is transfigured and idealised, and where the light which clothes the blessed is rather "a celestial radiance than a light," which "sustains them, proceeds from them, returns to them, pervades them, and incorporates them, and is, in truth, an inexhaustible source of peace and joy ; it is a fountain of delight in which they are absorbed, as fishes are absorbed in the sea." It is the same feeling that leads him to endow these blessed ones with pity for the miseries of men, only it is "a tender and peaceful pity which in nowise mars their immutable felicity " (Book XIV).

Is it necessary to refer to the style, the inherent qualities of which stand self-revealed in the preceding pages ? It may, however, be useful to enumerate its chief characteristics. The distinguishing feature of his style, in every one of Fénelon's works, but especially in *Télémaque*, is grace. No French prose writer comes up to him in this respect. No one has depicted sweet, pleasant, and natural things so well as Fénelon. When he describes nature, it is always in the simplest and most familiar colours. He paints admirable pictures of youth (Telemachus), the death of a young man (Hippias, and Pisistratus), the abode of the blessed in the Elysian Fields. Grace never departs from his style, even when it rises to solemnity or sublimity, as in the speech of Arcesius on old age, where it is allied with the loftiest melancholy ; sometimes it accompanies the subtlest metaphysical reasoning, for example, when, in accordance with St. John's Gospel, he speaks of " that simple, infinite, immutable light, which gives itself to everything without being divided."

FÉNELON

Besides grace, which, according to La Fontaine, is more beautiful than beauty itself, Fénelon is abundantly endowed with imagination, not, as in the case of Bossuet, of a grand, sublime, profound, and Hebraistic nature, but of a lively, brilliant, coloured, Greek type. His narrative, in the finest passages (battles, contests, shipwrecks), is rapid, and composed of restrained, animated, and striking expressions. Grace is not incompatible with energy (the combat of Adrastus and Telemachus), or with pathos (the sacrifice of Idomeneus), or with horror (the death of Bocchoris). He excels most, however, in the description of all things noble, refined, and pure. Unlike other poets, his picture of Paradise[1] is superior to the one he draws of Hell.

Finally, what are we to think of *Télémaque* ? It is difficult to see in it a composition of the first order, for it is not a work of creation and invention, but a series of imitations and literary reminiscences. Its greatest charm resides in the fact that it makes antiquity live again for us. We cannot place it on a level with the *Iliad*, and the *Aeneid*, nor even with Milton's *Paradise*

[1] *Cf.* Note liii, p. 282.

Lost, or Tasso's *Jerusalem Delivered*. Even Chateaubriand's *Martyrs*,[1] which is equally out of fashion, is a more original work. The description of the two civilisations, pagan and Christian, in their struggles and conflicts, is of more vivid interest than the search for Ulysses. The martyrdom of Cymodocea is more touching than the wanderings of Telemachus. Even the style, which is less limpid, and of an inferior epoch, possesses greater nobility and lustre. And yet no one to-day reads the *Martyrs ;* but then are there many who read *Télémaque ?* It is the fate of the masterpieces of the past, and especially of fiction, after the period of their first success, to be looked upon at a later date with cold and disdainful esteem. If the stage did not preserve our tragedies, they would probably share the same destiny. *Télémaque* is none the less a work of great beauty ; we have set forth its chief merits : among classical works of the second rank, none are worthier of their high reputation.

Are we then to endorse Bossuet's harsh and scornful judgment : [2] " Not a very

[1] *Cf*. Note li, p. 282.
[2] *Cf*. Note liv, p. 283.

serious work, and one hardly worthy of a
priest " ?   This opinion is unjust ; *Télémaque* is essentially a serious work, unless
we are to condemn all imaginative literature. Is it unworthy of a priest ? We
can say nothing on that point, not knowing
how far along the path of profane literature
a priest has the right to advance. One
thing is certain : there are no traces, however slight, of the ecclesiastical spirit, and
this is the great charm of the book. What
we esteem most in Fénelon is the fact that
he is not exclusively a priest, and that he
is able to forget his cloth for a time, in order
to divert himself, and to relate, for his own
edification, the adventures of his young
hero. He was so fond of romances that
he actually wrote one himself. Can we fail
to forgive him for this weakness ? He did
not shrink, he, an Archbishop, from por-
traying love on two occasions, in the form
of bewitching voluptuousness, and in the
shape of artless grace, in the persons of
Eucharis and Antiope. Not a word of
Bossuet's leads us to imagine that he himself understood the charm of innocent love.
In tragedies, he condemns even generous
love, and never sees any other side, save

the carnal. Fénelon has none of this mon-
astic distrust ; it is obvious that he smiles
benevolently on the early preludes of a
happy and virtuous marriage, and that he
does not forbid its tender caresses. All
this has something touchingly and delightfully human about it. *Télémaque* then is
not the work of a priest ; yet it would not
be so moving had it not been written by
a priest. We grant that Fénelon went
rather far for an Archbishop ; but we love
him none the less for that, on the contrary ;
and ecclesiastical censorship not being our
business, we absolve him in the name of
literary criticism.

CHAPTER VIII

FÉNELON AS POLITICAL THINKER

IT has often been asked whether Fénelon's political opinions were those of a really liberal politician, with his gaze turned towards the future, or if they were not rather of the nature of an echo, and a regret for the past, that is, for an aristocratic monarchy, under which the King's authority would have been kept in check solely by the privileges of the aristocracy.

In our opinion, this is an exaggerated view. Being a nobleman, and living in such an age, no doubt Fénelon did not dream of, nor would he have assented to, the weakening of the aristocracy ; just as Montesquieu himself regarded the nobility as an essential part of the monarchical government. But what does the greatest credit to Fénelon, and proves that his mind was turned towards the future as well as towards the past, is his keen perception of the need for the nation to participate in the royal authority. What he says, for example, about the inefficiency of despotism, is absolutely true ; and on more than one occasion, during the course of the national history of France, the truth and depth of Fénelon's statement have been confirmed by events.

"Our misfortune," he wrote in 1710 to his friend the Duke of Chevreuse,[1] "is that this war has only been, up till now, the concern of the King, who is ruined and discredited. It ought to be made the real business of the entire body of the nation. This it has become only too truly : peace having been broken, the bulk of the nation sees itself menaced with the peril of sub-jugation. . . . The whole of our nation should be intimately and constantly per-suaded, that it is the nation itself that bears the weight of this war, just as the English and Dutch are persuaded that it is by their own choice, and in their own interests, that they are waging war. I would have the raising of the necessary funds left to the wealthiest classes. At first, they would per-haps be unacquainted with the business. It is in order that they may be made conver-sant with it, that I would have them under-take this examination. Then each one would say to himself : this is no longer a

[1] *Cf. Correspondance*, i, p. 390.

matter of the past, it is a question of the future. *It is the duty of the nation to save itself.*"

Is it possible to maintain that the man who wrote such a page is not one of our ancestors, one of the forerunners of modern liberalism ? Did he not accurately foresee what has been termed the government of the people by the people ? The fact that he upheld, in what he calls the nation, the aristocratic element with its privileges, and that some utopian conceptions have found their way into his political schemes, in no way destroys the force and authority of the true principles he laid down.

The time was about to dawn when Fénelon would be called upon to draw up something more than theoretical and general plans of government, more akin to ethics than to politics. A day came when he appeared to be on the eve of having to take up the practical responsibility of applying his ideas. His Royal Highness was dead ; the Prince, who had been known as the Dauphin, throughout Louis XIV's reign, had died in 1711. His appointed successor, the new Dauphin, was the Duke of Burgundy, Fénelon's pupil. Nothing now stood between the young Duke and the crown of France but a broken and enfeebled old man whose demise seemed imminent. Fénelon's functions during the new reign were obvious. It was plainly requisite to draw up the plan of a new policy, in order not to be found unprepared. The little circle of the Duke of Burgundy, of the two Dukes, as it was called (the Duke of Beauvillier and the Duke of Chevreuse), naturally approached Fénelon on the matter. It would have been difficult to prepare such a plan in letters, so it was decided that the chief actors should meet face to face. A Conference was held at Chaulnes, in November, 1711, when long and important conversations took place, the results of which were embodied in short and concise maxims, chapter-headings, which Fénelon called *Tables*, and which are now known under the name of *Tables de Chaulnes*.[1] It is in these Tables that Fénelon approaches nearest to practical politics. Here we see the principles which he would have endeavoured to apply, if events had placed him at the head of the government. We must not expect more from him than was compatible with the times. His are not the

[1] *Cf. Œuvres*, xxii, Plans de gouvernement, p. 575.

Principles of 1789;[1] but if we go back in thought to the period when these rules were formulated, we shall see that they were the outcome of a spirit which was totally opposed to the doctrine of absolute monarchy, and to Louis XIV's government.

In the first place, he urged the reform of the Court; here Fénelon was striking at the gravest evil of all and the hardest to uproot, at the occult power which, at a later date, thwarted and overthrew Turgot,[2] and which, by its blind opposition, helped to transform '89 into '93, I mean the ascendancy of the Court. From the very first lines, and without suspecting it, Fénelon suggests a revolution : " Suppression of all unnecessary pensions. Exclusion of all useless favours. Moderation in furniture and apparel. A truce to building. Reduction in the number of State apartments. Suspension of all cumulative functions." This clearly meant war against the whole Court. How could this plan be successfully carried through without the support of the people ? We see that, at the very outset of these reforms, a revolution was in the making.

[1] *Cf.* Note lv, p. 284.
[2] *Cf.* Note lvi, p. 284.

To believe in the possibility of such reforms, one must have studied politics in *Télémaque*. And yet this very reform of the Court was the first condition of salvation for the monarchy.

But it is mainly in the sphere of politics, and in all that concerns the participation of the people in the government, that the liberal bias of Fénelon's plan appears most clearly. For he calls for a return to the States-General, to what he terms the " Parliament of the entire Kingdom." He affirms that they will be " peaceful and loyal like those of Languedoc and Brittany," etc. Doubtless, the composition of these States still savours somewhat of the middle ages. The Bishop of each Diocese is a member *ex officio ;* but the representative of the nobility is elected like the deputy of the Tiers-État. The question of the suppression of the three orders is not yet raised ; no one thought of such a thing at the time. But the vital point was that the elections were to be free : " Freedom of election : the King to offer no advice, which, in practice had always meant an order." The States were to assemble every three years in an appointed town, and were to continue their deliberations as long as might be deemed necessary. This was tantamount to permanency. They were to be empowered to extend their inquiries over all questions pertaining to justice, policy, finance, war, alliances and maritime law, agriculture and commerce. In a word, the whole field of politics was open to them. Moreover, they had authority " to punish lawless lords."

The distinction between the temporal and the spiritual powers was established with just discrimination. Fénelon approves of the Gallican liberties,[1] in so far as the past is concerned, but as regards the present, he sees in them nothing but an extension of the King's despotic power : " In former times, Rome exhibited a most arbitrary authority ; but her initiative is now greatly curtailed. To-day, the power of initiation emanates from the secular authority ; freedom, in relation to the Pope, servitude, to the King. The laity predominate over the Bishops : there is an abuse of appeals by writ of error, and it is a bad custom to allow laymen to examine Bulls touching matters of faith." Fénelon conceives of a system

[1] *Cf.* Note xli, p. 277.

which is not far removed from what we to-day should call the separation of Church and State. In fact, as an example of the situation which he desiderates for the Catholic Church, he quotes the case of the early Protestant Churches of France, which " appointed pastors, assembled the faithful, administered their own affairs, and excommunicated, without the intervention of the secular power." He ardently desires for the Catholic Church the liberty she enjoys in Holland and Turkey : " The Grand Turk leaves the Christians free to elect and depose their pastors. If the Church of France were placed in the same position, there would be a freedom, which does not now exist, to elect, depose, assemble. . . . The King is a layman. The Church can excommunicate the Sovereign ; the Sovereign can kill the pastor. The Church has no right to establish or to depose Kings."

Of course, Fénelon does not go to the length of secularising the State. He is not opposed to a State religion, and he says absolutely nothing about liberty of conscience ; nevertheless, his religious policy, like his secular policy, is a kind of forecast of the future. As in all his other writings, he exhibits, in this domain also, an independent and reforming spirit, a concern for liberty, and enthusiasm for a measure of individuality, at least to the separate existence of the various bodies, to the sovereignty of the nation, and to its intervention in the State. Even his political economy is somewhat liberal in tendency : "France is rich enough, if she sells her wheat, her oil, her wine, her cloth, etc., in a good market. From England and Holland, she will buy spices and matchless curiosities. *Allow freedom of trade.*" [1] The total effect, however, is slightly marred by recollections of *Télémaque :* "Sumptuary laws should be made for every condition of life ; as it is, the nobles are being ruined in order to enrich the trading class ; luxury corrupts the nation's morals, and there is greater mischief in luxury, than utility in the profits which accrue from fashion."

There is undoubtedly enough in all these projects to justify, in a certain measure, the saying of Louis XIV concerning Fénelon, that he was "the most visionary man of genius in his Kingdom." Yes, this is true ; but, at the same time, it must be added :

[1] *Cf.* Note lvii, p. 284.

the noblest and most enlightened, and the one nearest to us by his outlook towards better things, and by his faith in progress, although he still belongs to the society of the past by some of his prejudices.

While Fénelon was endowed with a keen sense of the rights of the people, he held equally strong views concerning the duties of Kings. He has left a striking exposition of these duties, in his *Examen de conscience des devoirs de la royauté.*[1] This work does not contain the commonplace and monotonous moral statements of *Télémaque*, which seem to be designed for children, rather than for fullgrown men. It is a real and concrete treatment of political ethics; it presents urgent and definite advice, together with many bold allusions to Louis XIV; it was to be perused in secret by the Duke of Burgundy: for what would the Grand Roi have said of such unpalatable moral teaching?

In Xenophon, we see Socrates indoctrinating an ambitious young man, Glaucon,

---

[1] *Cf. Œuvres*, xxii, p. 255. This work had been published previously under the title of *Direction pour la conscience d'un roi;* it is better known under the latter title.

who was desirous of engaging in public affairs, without having any knowledge of the real interests and political situation of the State. With ruthless irony, Socrates brings home to him his incompetency and powerlessness : "Do you know," says Socrates to the youth, "the number of soldiers who are fit for service, the fortresses and arsenals, the revenues and taxes, the laws and tribunals ? " etc. ; and to each of these questions, Glaucon is obliged to reply that he has not yet had time to look into them. It is by a similar process of questioning that Fénelon approaches the Duke of Burgundy. He reminds him of the manifold obligations which devolve upon the head of a State, and of the vast knowledge which his functions demand : "Have you made it your business," he asks him, "to become acquainted with the laws, customs, and usages of the Kingdom ? The King is the sovereign judge ; now, to be a good judge is to judge according to the laws. These must be known. Do you know them, and are you in a position to point out an error to a judge who is ignorant of the laws ? " But it is not everything to know the laws. There are also institutions, even under an absolute monarchy : " Have you studied the real strength of the government of your country ? Have you sought to find out what are the limits of your authority ? Do you know what forms of government prevailed under the different Dynasties, and what the ancient Parliaments were, as well as the States-General which have succeeded them ? " As we see, Fénelon never loses sight of the national institutions, which in earlier times limited the power of the King, but recalls them to the mind of the young heir to the throne. He further bids him endeavour to understand " the essence of anarchy and of despotism, and also of constitutional monarchy, which is the middle course between the other two."[1] Then comes more positive information, similar to that proffered by Socrates to Glaucon : the number of men, women, husbandmen, artisans, traders, priests, nobles, and soldiers in the nation ; the nature of the inhabitants, their customs, immunities, commerce, laws regarding trade, tribunals, and the rights and abuses of taxation.

We are not surprised to find that Fénelon

[1] *Cf.* Note lviii, p. 285.

deals severely with war.[2] This attitude
colours the whole of his policy: "There
never was a war," he says, "even a successful war, which did not cause more harm
than good to the State: we have only to
consider how many families it ruins, how
many men it kills, how it lays waste and
depopulates all countries, and how it author-
ises licence." It is not enough to avoid
war: when one has been forced to resort
to its arbitrament, one must remain faithful
to the agreement by which it was ended:
"Have you been faithful in keeping your
undertaking? There are laws of warfare
which must be observed with no less loyalty
than the laws of peace. There is the law
of nations, which is the foundation of
humanity itself; it is a sacred and inviolable bond between the peoples. Have you
scrupulously carried out the provisions of
the peace treaties? Have you never violated
them under specious pretences?"

Finally, the work closes with excellent
advice concerning the knowledge of men,
and the choice of ministers, the attitude
to be observed towards them, the wrong
use of favourites, etc.; all this is the fruit

[1] *Cf.* Note lix, p. 285.

of wise and enlightened experience, and is justified by the examples of all times ; the study of this work would not be unprofitable even to-day, under a wholly different form of government.

There is a very close link between the *Examen de conscience* and the famous *Lettre à Louis XIV*, that extraordinary Letter which is so bold, uncompromising, and lacking in respect towards the King, that many have doubted its authenticity.[1] It was difficult to believe that a subject, a priest, and a subordinate could ever have spoken with such utter fearlessness. It is true the Letter was anonymous. The author concealed his rank and name, and declared that he was not known to the King, and that he expected nothing from him. In spite of these evasions and subterfuges, the attack is so vehement that it was long thought, as I have said, that the Letter was apocryphal and a forgery. But all doubts and difficulties had perforce to vanish in presence of the autograph manuscript which is still in existence to-day. " This manuscript," it is said in the great edition of Fénelon's works " was purchased by Renouard, the publisher, on

[1] *Cf.* Note lxxxv, p. 292.

February 24, 1825, at the sale of books of the late M. Gentil, and he immediately issued a very careful edition, with a facsimile of the first page."[1]

Its authenticity is therefore beyond all doubt, but other questions have been raised. Was this Letter ever delivered to Louis XIV ? The Marquis of Fénelon, the Archbishop's nephew, thought he could vouch for it. According to him, " the Letter was handed to the King by the Duke of Beauvillier, and the King, far from taking offence, shortly afterwards chose Fénelon as Tutor to his grandchildren." But an anachronism renders this assertion inadmissible : Fénelon was appointed Tutor in 1689, and internal evidence proves conclusively that the Letter was written at a date subsequent at least to 1691. Moreover, how can we admit that the Duke of Beauvillier was requested to deliver, in person, a Letter in which he was himself very severely taken to task, and in which it was stated that " his weakness and timidity were a dishonour to himself, and a scandal to society " ? For the same reason, it is impossible to believe that Mme. de Maintenon ever set eyes on this Letter,

[1] *Cf. Œuvres* de Fénelon, *Correspondance*, ii, p. 329.

since she is included in the same sentences with the Duke of Beauvillier, as dishonouring herself and scandalising society by her cowardliness. And yet, to what other Letter could she be referring, when she wrote to the Archbishop of Paris (December 21, 1691): " Here is a Letter addressed to him (the King) two or three years ago. It is well written ; but such truths cannot avail to reclaim him, they only irritate and discourage him. Do you not recognise the style ? " It is not easy to suppose that these words can refer to any Letter, other than Fénelon's, and yet the difficulty alluded to above still remains. The conclusion generally drawn from these facts is that the original in our possession is a rough draft, subsequently modified by Fénelon, who deleted all references to Mme. de Maintenon and the Duke of Beauvillier. We find it hard to believe that the Letter, even thus modified, was ever actually delivered to the King, and the reasons mentioned by Mme. de Maintenon are adequate to explain the motives for which it was withheld.[1]

Whatever the truth of the matter, the

[1] *Cf.* Note lx, p. 285.

following are the chief points in this Letter, which might be termed a pamphlet, if it were not addressed directly to the person of the King, and with a great display of " zeal, loyalty, and personal feeling."

What Fénelon lays special stress upon, and what constitutes his fundamental thought, as we have already seen, is that the rule of Louis XIV had degenerated into despotism and absolutism : " All your Ministers," he says, " have entirely destroyed the ancient maxims of the State, in order that your authority might be carried to its utmost limits. Mention is no longer made of the State, or of rulés : they talk only of the King and his good pleasure ; they have extolled you to the skies." But this absolutism is only an empty show : the real power is entirely in the hands of the Ministers of State : " You have thought to govern, by assigning limits to those who governed. The latter have shown themselves merciless, haughty, unjust, violent, and dishonest."

Fénelon's severest indictment of the King is on the score of his abuse of war ; he traces the origin of all the misfortunes which have fallen on the Kingdom, to the war against Holland : " They led your Majesty to undertake the war against Holland for your glory, and in order to punish the Dutch for having given vent to some jesting re-marks. . . . The only ground of this war lay in a motive of glory, or of vengeance, and such a motive is insufficient to justify a war."

What were the effects of this policy on the inner condition of the Kingdom ? Fénelon traces an awful picture of the state of France at this time (1691) :[1] " Your subjects are dying of hunger ; the cultivation of the soil is practically abandoned, all business is at a standstill, commerce is entirely ruined. France has become a huge hospital. The magistrates are discredited and harassed. . . . You alone have brought all this trouble upon yourself ; for, the whole King-dom having been ruined, you now hold everything in your own hands, and no one can so much as live, save by your bounty." Nay more, the people were losing their faith and loyalty. We seem to be on the eve of the Revolution, when we hear Fénelon uttering such words as these : " The people who once loved you so deeply are beginning

[1] *Cf.* Note lxi, p. 285.

to lose affection, confidence, and even re-spect. They no longer rejoice at your vic-tories; they are filled with bitterness and despair. Sedition·is being kindled little by little on all sides."

Finally, how could Fénelon give expres-sion to thoughts such as the following, in the presence of Louis XIV, who prided himself so much on his religious zeal : " You do not love God ; even your fear of Him is a slavish fear. It is Hell you dread. Your religion consists only of superstitions, and little superficial practices. You make everything centre round your own person, as if you were the God of the whole earth." These were very cruel words : was it wise or humane to address the King in such bitter and unmeasured terms ? It is not surprising that Mme. de Maintenon should have deemed the Letter too strong ; even after it had been greatly toned down, as doubtless it was, perhaps it was still too severe. However that may be, the man who wrote in this strain considered things as they were viewed at the end of the reign, and at the close of the following century. He was anticipating the terrible lesson which history was about to give to Kings. Had these truths, cruel or not, been listened to in time, they might perchance have warded off the blows of destiny. What cannot be denied is that Fénelon perceived, before anyone else, the evils of despotism which were undermining the monarchy, and that he was one of those who remained undazzled by the brilliance of the glorious reign. Such clear-sightedness at the Court itself, and in the midst of the universal dazzlement, reveals a mind of no ordinary calibre.

In order to give a complete survey of Fénelon's political outlook, we should need to follow him on the field of practical politics, that is to say, in his *Lettres* and *Mémoires* concerning the affairs of the Spanish Succession.[1] In the latter, it is no longer a matter of general plans, and more or less ideal reforms ; Fénelon is dealing with real and daily facts and occurrences, upon which he gives his opinion with great precision and firmness. Here he does not show himself a visionary politician, as he had done in his description of Salentum, but a practical politician, at times even too practical, for in moments of discouragement, he urges peace in spite of everything, and at any

[1] *Cf. Œuvres*, xxii, p. 467.

price. On this occasion, it was Louis XIV who was the visionary, and who was in the right. He saved France, and prevented her being humiliated. Nevertheless, Fénelon's Memoir to the Duke of Beauvillier, in 1701, *Sur les moyens de prévenir la guerre*, reveals a wise, shrewd, and well-informed policy.

CHAPTER IX

FÉNELON'S PHILOSOPHY

It is known in a general way that Fénelon busied himself with philosophical problems, and that he wrote a *Traité de l'Existence de Dieu*, the literary passages of which are chiefly remembered to-day. But it is not known that he is one of the keenest and boldest thinkers in the literature of French philosophy; his highest flights in metaphysics, for example in the second part of the *Existence de Dieu*, are closely related to the subtleties and sublimities of his theology.

Fénelon's philosophical works are three in number: 1. *Réfutation du traité du P. Malebranche sur la nature et la grâce;*[1] 2. *Traité de l'Existence de Dieu;* 3. *Lettres sur divers sujets de religion et de métaphysique.* Since the last named work offers little interest, we will leave it on one side; we will also pass by the first, for the reason that it is too technical, and that it concerns the expert, rather than the general, reader;

[1] First published in the great edition of 1827, vol. i.

we will therefore lay special emphasis on
the *Traité de l'Existence de Dieu*.

This treatise is not a controversial work ;
it is a dogmatic essay, containing a complete metaphysic. It comprises two parts,
which are really two distinct works. The
first part was written in Fénelon's earlier
life, according to the testimony of Ramsay ;
it is a work of an essentially popular character and of a literary form, except at the
end. The second part is, in reality, a metaphysical treatise of high import. The author
boldly adopts the system of methodical
doubt, which he carries to its furthest
limits ; he expounds only the metaphysical
proofs of the existence of God, and rises
to the loftiest and most abstruse doctrines.
One part only of the work was published
during Fénelon's lifetime, in 1712, but without his knowledge. It was only in 1718
that the two parts were bound together in
a single work, under the editorship of Ramsay and the Marquis of Fénelon. This
edition was very inaccurate, owing either
to negligence, or to the scruples of the editors,
who treated Fénelon in the same way as
Port-Royal treated Pascal.[1]

[1] *Cf.* Note lxii, p. 286.

FÉNELON'S PHILOSOPHY

The first part of the *Existence de Dieu* is better known than the second ; it long remained a classic of the schoolroom. It is an eloquent work, written in copious and magnificent language, and one in which Fénelon has sought the inspiration of the Ancients, expounding the celebrated argument from final causes,[1] and, in a more modern form, the argument based on the marvels of nature. Fénelon has chiefly imitated Cicero's *De Natura Deorum*, a work which propounded the doctrine of the Stoics, who, while they did not initiate the argument from final causes, which dates back to Socrates, nevertheless gave it its greatest development. This argument is composed of what is known in logic as a major and a minor premise. The following proposition constitutes the major : " everything that reveals order, and well-regulated art, is the work of intelligence." The minor is to the effect that : " nature, in all her works, reveals order and art." The conclusion is that " nature has an intelligent cause." That is the epitome of the argument which Bossuet gives in his *Connaissance de Dieu et de soi-même* (Chap. IV, 1).

[1] *Cf.* Note lxiii, p. 286.

FÉNELON

Fénelon's first chapter, which is very short, contains an exposition of the major. This first premise is, so to speak, a truth of common sense, and it was illustrated by the Ancients, with the aid of ingenious comparisons which Fénelon reproduces, for example, the improbability of lighting upon the poem of the *Iliad*, or even the first line of that poem, by throwing the letters of the alphabet haphazard ; the impossibility of painting a picture by casting, at random, a brush filled with paint on a canvas : at most, the foam of a horse might be obtained thus, as legend relates of Apelles ; the absolute certainty with which it might be affirmed, on coming across statues and monuments in a deserted island, that the island had been inhabited by men, and that these were evidences of the operation of the mind, etc. ; all these reasons, which are only figures, are nevertheless proofs which help us to realise the truth of the axiom upon which all are agreed, when dealing with human works : why should not the axiom be extended ,to the whole realm of nature ?

The second chapter is the longest in the work, for it is made up of all the facts which go to prove that there is order in nature. In the exposition of these facts, Fénelon follows a kind of ascending scale ; he proceeds from the simplest to the most complex, from the less perfect to the more perfect. According to the method pursued in physics during the middle ages, he begins with what were known as the elements : earth, fire, water, etc. Next, he passes on to the stars. Then, returning to the earth, he deals with living beings, and in particular with the animals, concerning whom he makes some very ingenious observations. In the mechanism of the animal, he notes that : 1st, this mechanism is capable of defending itself against those who attack it with a view to destroying it ; 2nd, it is capable of renewing itself by means of nourishment ; 3rd, it is capable of perpetuating its species by generation. "What would be thought of a watch, which should run away when necessary, recoil, defend itself, and make its escape, in order to preserve its life ? What could be more beautiful than a machine which repairs and renews itself continually ? What should we say of a watchmaker who knew how to make watches, which of themselves produced an endless series of new ones, so that the two first sufficed to multiply the species ? "

From animals in general, Fénelon passes on to man ; and he describes first his bodily functions, then the faculties of his soul. At this point, he ascends the scale of the faculties, and, starting from the senses and memory, he mounts up to reason and ideas, that is to say, to those eternal and universal truths which are known to all men, in every place, and in all climes, and which are a sort of emanation from the divine reason.

The argument here assumes a different character. It is no longer the physical proof from final causes : it is the metaphysical and Platonic argument founded on the ideas. "There are," says Fénelon, " two kinds of reason in me : the one is myself, the other is above me ; the one that is me is very imperfect, defective, unreliable, biassed, hasty, changeable, and stubborn ; in a word, it possesses nothing but borrowed elements ; the other is common to all men, perfect, eternal, immutable, ever ready to impart itself, and to restore a right judgment, incapable of ever being exhausted or divided. Where is this perfect reason, which is so close to me, yet so different from me ?

It must be something substantial. Where does this supreme reason dwell? *Is it not the God I am seeking?*"

These last words of the first part already announce the thoughts of the second; they possess the same merits, namely, glowing and sublime eloquence in the realm of abstractions. In this order of ideas, Fénelon is the equal of Malebranche as regards style, but with perhaps even more warmth and enthusiasm.

As to the long disquisition on the marvels of nature, which fills the second chapter of this first part, it is a fine imitation of the Ancients, although perhaps not quite worthy of modern science. Fénelon had not studied science, and it is impossible to treat profitably of the order of the universe, without some scientific knowledge. So it happens that, in places, he is at fault. For example, when he speaks thus: "Who hath suspended this round earth which is *immovable?*" This is to ignore too flagrantly the great discovery of Copernicus and Galileo. He does not hesitate to say that " the sun moves round us for the express purpose of serving man." He shows that the moon was made in order to give us light; and yet it lights us only during a quarter of the month, and the remainder of the time it leaves us in darkness; moreover, astronomers have taken upon themselves to tell us what God would have needed to have done, for the moon to perform the functions which are wrongly attributed to it. Fénelon himself raises the objection that all these things are governed by immutable laws. He replies: "I suppose the fact." Was it permissible, at the end of the seventeenth century, after Kepler, Galileo, Descartes, and Newton, to advance as a mere supposition and concession, that there are laws in nature? Furthermore, Fénelon carries the argument from final causes too far, principally in the direction already condemned by Descartes, by referring everything to man, as to the exclusive end of nature. He states, for example, that the Ocean was created in order to be a means of communication between the different continents; yet, if there were no Ocean, the continents would be in natural communication with each other, since they would be all one; "yes," he says, "but with incredible fatigue": doubtless, but then is the Ocean less dangerous?

In a word, this part of the book is the work of too inaccurate a mind, and one too little acquainted with the exact methods of science. It is worth while to compare Fénelon's work, in this respect, with Bossuet's on *La Connaissance de Dieu et de soi-même*. Bossuet also touches on scientific questions, at least of anatomy and physiology ; but in order to deal with these subjects competently, and with a knowledge of the facts, he had attended, during a whole winter, the lectures of Sténon, a celebrated anatomist of the time. So it comes that the chapter in Bossuet's work which treats of the body, is a correct and faithful, albeit elementary, epitome of the science of his day.[1]

In our analysis of the second part of the *Existence de Dieu*, we will omit everything which is a mere reproduction of the Cartesian method and doctrines. Fénelon follows Descartes step by step, with more subtlety, but less cogency. His is the same

[1] In order to be quite fair, we must state that the eminent naturalist, Georges Pouchet, assures us that the passage in Fénelon which deals with nutrition (*Œuvres*, i, p. 38), is in perfect harmony with modern science, and even marks an advance on Bossuet.

methodical doubt, the *Cogito, ergo sum*, the principle of evidence, the proof of the existence of God based on the imperfection of human beings, on the conception we have of the infinite, on the idea of a necessary Being. Finally comes the proof, not Cartesian, but Platonic, founded on the nature of the ideas, the proof with which the first part closed. We will pass by these doctrines, and will only draw attention to those which connect Fénelon, not with Descartes, or even Plato, but with the Neo-Platonism of Alexandria. It is obviously to this source that we must trace his doctrine of the absolute unity of God : his views on this point are profoundly original, and even practically unique in French philosophy.[1]

For Fénelon, as for Descartes, God is the infinitely perfect Being. But, if we say *Being*, is it necessary to add *perfect*, or even *infinite ?* He is the Being above all others, essential Being, in one word, Being, " without qualification." He is therefore perfectly one : one is better than many. He is one, simple, without component parts, division, number, or succession. His is perfect unity, equivalent to perfect multitude, or infinitely

[1] *Cf.* Note lxiv, p. 286.

surpassing it. Since He is the first Being, " He must be conceived of as All, not as *plures*, but as *plus omnibus*. In virtue and perfection, that is, " intensively," He possesses what He cannot have in multiplication and extent, that is, " extensively."

In the case of all finite beings without exception, it may be said that they are this or that. Nothing of the sort can be said of the infinite Being. To be precisely one certain thing, is to be only that thing in particular. When I have stated of the infinite Being that He is simply Being, without adding any epithet, I have said everything. His difference is that He possesses none. The word infinite gives Him nothing in effect : it is almost a superfluous term.

As it is not possible to define God in a precise manner without confining Him within certain limits, " He is not more spirit than body, nor body than spirit. He is the real and positive part of all bodies and spirits," the only reality and substance in the essential elements of all possible creatures. Remove all limits and differences, and you remain in the universality of Being. When

Moses refers to God, he does not say : He Who is spirit ; but he says : He Who is. He Who is spirit, is only spirit ; He Who is, is the totality of Being.

We therefore understand that there cannot be several infinities. To say *several* is to signify an augmentation of our being. Several infinities would be infinitely less than one. That which is composite is made up of parts, of which one is not the other. Every composite body is, therefore, a number that can never constitute the supreme unity, which is the only real infinite : " by multiplying the unity, you diminish it."

How was it possible for creation to emanate from this supreme unity ? What were the ideas according to which God created the world ? What were the eternal patterns upon which, according to Plato and his school, God gazed in the act of creating ? Fénelon answers this query as follows :

God, being absolute perfection, contains within Himself, in His essence, " an infinite number of degrees of perfection : these degrees of perfection are the norm and prototype of an infinite variety of possible creatures."

How can there be degrees in the infinite

and absolutely perfect Being ? These are merely modes of speech : " Finite, ignorant man always stammers when he speaks of the infinite Being." In reality, " these degrees have no separate identity. They are indivisible ; but what is inseparable in God is capable of division in creatures. As the essential characteristic of the infinite Being is to create being, the created being is of itself susceptible of degrees, being essentially finite." " The Being who exists infinitely, beholds, rising to infinity, all the degrees to which he can impart being. Each degree of possible communication constitutes a possible essence which corresponds to a degree of being, which in God is inseverable from all other degrees. Here is the source of the universals, the genera, and the species : here are the changeless patterns of the works of God."

The individual remains to be explained. Here Fénelon fails, like all other philosophers. He is forced to confuse individuality with what he terms " actual existence."— " Actual existence," he says, " is precisely what distinguishes one thing from another. The actual existence of my neighbour is not mine : the one is entirely independent of the other. He may cease to be, without my existence being jeopardised. This independence shows the real separateness, and is the only true difference between individuals." This doctrine does not appear to us to shed much light on the conception of individuality : for if an individual be not already distinct in himself, his actual existence is absolutely identical with the actual existence of another individual. We must therefore revert to the position of accepting the individual as a fact, without any further explanation.

Now how is the absolute oneness of God to be reconciled with the multiplicity of the divine attributes ? Just as our mind thinks it can distinguish degrees in the absolute unity of divine perfection, so it imagines it can discover various and manifold perfections, where there is only one absolute indivisibility : " I picture this unique Being to myself in His different aspects, and, as it were, according to the divers relations in which He stands to His works. These are what we call perfections or attributes. I give different names to the same thing, according to its external relationships ; but I do not claim, by these various names, to be predicating really different things. God is infinitely wise, infinitely powerful, infinitely good; but His wisdom, power, and goodness are merely one and the same thing. That in Him which thinks is the same thing as that which wills; that which acts, and has power to do everything, is precisely the same thing as that which thinks and wills; that which upholds is identical with that which destroys; that which punishes is one with that which forgives. In a word, in Him all is one in perfect unity. This distinction between the divine perfections, which I assume when I consider God, possesses, therefore, no reality in Him, but is an order and a method, which I must perforce adopt in the consecutive and limited operations of my mind, in order, so to speak, to store my knowledge, and that I may contemplate the Infinite in successive stages, considering Him from the point of view of the different things He performs outside Himself."

One cannot help inquiring how so bold a doctrine can be reconciled with the Christian dogma of the Trinity, how a plurality of divine Persons can be understood in a Being absolutely one, of transcendent unity.

Shall we say that it is the human mind that distinguishes the divine Persons, in order to proportion the divine nature to the human? Is not this tantamount to destroying the reality of the divine Persons considered in themselves, and therefore to drying up Christianity at its source? Or perhaps it will be said that this is a question of faith which does not concern philosophy? The fact remains that the Trinity introduces multiplicity into the Godhead, and that there can be no more talk about absolute unity. Faith would then be revealing to us a God in Whom plurality reappears, although the idea of absolute perfection seems to exclude all plurality. We do not know whether Fénelon was conscious of these difficulties, nor how he succeeded in solving them for himself. At all events, we find that, both in metaphysics and in theology, his doctrine verges on heresy, however sincerely anxious he may have been not to lapse into it.

Still, with what marvellous and sublime eloquence he speaks of this supreme and inaccessible unity!

" O manifold creation, how poor thou art in thy seeming abundance! Numbers are soon exhausted. Only unity abides : it alone is everything, and beside it there is nothing. Complexity is only an illusion of being. It is an indescribable something which melts in my hands as soon as I press it. O God ! Thou alone art ! As for me, I am not ! O, who will deliver me from numbers, complexities, and successions, which savour so strongly of nothingness ? . . . They are magnificent numbers which seem to herald the units that form them ; but these units will never be found. The successive numbers are ever passing ; the number we are speaking of is already gone ; to seek it, is to have lost it. The next which is advancing does not yet exist. And yet, it is this multitude of nonentities that I call *me ;* it contemplates Being ; it divides it into parts, in order to contemplate it, and, in so doing, it acknowledges that the many cannot contemplate the indivisible One."

CHAPTER X

FÉNELON AS LITERARY CRITIC

In literary criticism, Fénelon is a master of the first order. An amiable and sprightly imagination, a lively appreciation of all that is pure, refined, unaffected, spontaneous, and homely, an exquisite feeling for antiquity, a mind eminently open towards new horizons—all these qualities are evidences of an innate genius for criticism. Boileau, doubtless, possesses unerring and highly cultivated taste ; but he is very austere, and somewhat dry. Voltaire is exceedingly intelligent, but grandeur is beyond him : Corneille and Pascal fill him with amazement and dismay. La Harpe is learned, grave, and shrewd, but he is longwinded and tiresome. Vauvenargues alone presents some analogy with Fénelon, and belongs to the same class ; he is, however, somewhat too concise. Fénelon endows criticism with a grace, a freshness, and a native simplicity almost amounting to poetry. In his case, even the quotations reveal a happy turn of imagination, and a spirit of discernment and delicacy, which are not to be found in any other critic.

What we have just said is especially true of the *Lettre à l'Académie Française*.[1] The *Dialogues sur l'Éloquence* possess less charm, and at times are even lacking in discrimination. We propose to dwell chiefly on the former work.

In the *Lettre à l'Académie*, Fénelon shows himself, as he had done in the *Éducation des Filles*, a liberal, and at the same time somewhat of a politician. His political wisdom, for example, appears in connection with the Quarrel of the Ancients and the Moderns, when he argues both for and against, with such impartiality that it is difficult to say to which side he belongs, although in the main his heart is with the Ancients. Maybe this was not policy at all ; perhaps his mind was in all sincerity equally divided. For Fénelon is both a reactionary and an innovator ; he is passionately fond of antiquity, and he has at the same time a love of novelty. He believes that French poetry, eloquence, and history are capable of progressing, and he is anxious not to discourage them by a

[1] *Cf.* Note lxv, p. 286.

blind and superstitious admiration for the Ancients. Moreover, his Christianity refuses to confine its ideal to antiquity, so inferior to us both in ethical and religious conceptions. Hence, apart from all political considerations, that indecision and eclectic balancing of opinions which we find in the last chapter of the *Lettre à l'Académie*. In the body of the work, on the other hand, Fénelon constantly contrasts ancient and modern taste, giving the palm unmistakably to the former.

Let us, however, examine the work from the beginning. He treats first of the question of vocabulary and grammar, and does not side unreservedly with Malherbe's reform : " It seems to me," he says, "that during the past hundred years or so, the language has been obstructed and impoverished, in the attempt to purify it. It was still, undoubtedly, rather formless and too prolix ; yet, we cannot but regret the old style of Marot, Amyot, Cardinal d'Ossat, alike in the most playful and serious works. It possessed an indescribable element of terseness, native ingenuousness, boldness, vivacity, and passion." Fénelon does not mention Rabelais and Montaigne, though doubtless he had these writers in mind. Fénelon is thus keenly aware of all that the somewhat stilted speech of the seventeenth century has displaced ; but he appears too prone to believe that it is possible to improve a language at will. Thus he proposes, either to form compound words, after the manner of the Greeks and Romans, forgetting that Ronsard's attempt in this direction had proved a ludicrous failure ; or to borrow words from foreign languages, a thing which it is scarcely possible to do, except for technical purposes. It is true he deprecates excess and abuse ; he therefore thinks it right that this delicate work of neology should be entrusted not to the common herd, but to " persons of taste." Now, it is precisely the common herd that make languages ; and if the French Academy may sometimes have sufficient authority to forbid the use of certain words, it can never possess the power necessary to introduce new ones.[1] But it belongs to the great writer to make use of the accepted words ; his is the art " of combining terms, which are not ordinarily placed side by side."

As regards eloquence, Fénelon gives a

[1] *Cf.* Note lxvi, p. 287.

rapid summary of what he explains elsewhere in his *Dialogues sur l'Éloquence*. We
will return to this later. Let us pass on
to his views concerning poetry. He is severe
towards French poetry, and he has a clear
vision of its imperfections. Rhyme, in particular, appears to him a requirement more
injurious than useful. It forces the poet
to lengthen out his poem unduly, and " to
write two or three stop-gap lines, in order
to usher in the one he requires." He would
willingly say with Musset :

> Non, je ne connais pas de métier plus honteux,
> Plus sot, plus dégradant pour la cervelle humaine,
> Que d'écrire trois mots quand il n'en faut que deux.

Instead of preconising rich rhymes, like
the Parnassians of our day, he pleads, on
the contrary, for greater freedom. He complains of the monotony due to the repeti-
tion of the final syllables, which renders
the heroic poem so tedious, and he prefers
" the alternate rhymes, which La Fontaine
has so ably employed." He also recommends the use of inversions; he is not so
hard as Boileau on Ronsard's poetry, nor
does he blame him for having endeavoured
to enrich poetic diction, but only for having
attempted too much at once, and for not

having taken sufficiently into account the tastes and genius of the nation.

Another reproach which he levels against French poetry, (and in this he is inspired by his predilection for antiquity), is its straining after wit. He recommends un-affected graces, simple and artless beauty : no flashes of lightning, but rather a soft light, and homely and natural sublimity. The Ancients did not hesitate to put before us a shepherd with his flock, a nurse with a little child. Titian paints goat-herds ; Teniers, rustic festivities. Good Eumæus is more touching than Clœlia. Consider, in Virgil, the pathetic picture of a dying young man, Nisus and Euryalus, the loss of Eurydice, the plague among the animals, and, in Homer, Priam at the feet of Achilles. True grandeur consists in adapting one-self to one's subject. " It is not the elaborate and the exceptional that I seek, but the beautiful, expressed simply, attractively, and appropriately." In a word, what Fénelon loves in poetry is his own genius. The ideal he portrays, some idea of which we may gather from several passages in *Télémaque*, is a kind of blend of Racine, La Fontaine, and André Chénier.

Such are his views on poetry in general ;
let us now inquire into his particular opinions
concerning tragedy and comedy. Here it
must be admitted that his priestly office
hinders him a little from duly appreciating
all the beauties in our classics ; but he is
entirely justified in deploring the exaggerated part played by love in French tragedy.
The superiority, or, if you will, the originality of ancient drama, lies in the fact that
it succeeded in speaking directly to the
soul, without any appeal to the passions.
Among the Greeks, tragedy was independent of profane love. Could anything be
more ridiculous than to introduce love into
the tragic subject of Oedipus, as Corneille
has done ? Fénelon censures even Racine
for this. He blames him for having represented Hippolytus as in love, contrary to
tradition. " Phædra should have been left
alone in her frenzy. The action would have
been unique, short, and rapid." Yes ; but
we should have lost the jealousy scene !
Although some of these criticisms are plau-
sible enough, the following judgment on
our dramatists is rather severe : " Our poets
have given us plays which are as languishing, insipid, and sentimental as novels. They

deal with naught else save the fires, chains, and torments of love. They talk of dying, while in the best of health. All the characters are overdrawn, and nothing betokens real passion." All this is very harsh ; Hermione, Roxana, and Phædra are victorious replies to these strictures. Corneille himself, although he does undoubtedly often make an excessive use of the language of gallantry, has portrayed genuine passion in the *Cid*, and it is doing him an injustice to judge him by his *Oedipe*. He does, without question, lay himself open to censure by his fondness for declamation, and the first lines of *Cinna*, placed in the mouth of Émilie, are admittedly badly written ; but Fénelon does not seem sufficiently alive to the manly and heroic aspects of the old poet's genius. Fénelon was also the first, it would seem, to criticise the famous narrative of Theramenes,[1] which he thinks out of place and too lengthy ; yet those who have heard this narrative on the stage, know that it always creates a great impression, and that it is indeed most touching. But what Fénelon worships is Greek simplicity. He contrasts this long speech with the despair of Oedipus,

[1] *Cf.* Note lxvii, p. 287.

which, he says, is hardly anything but a lamentation and a cry. A little more, and he would reach Diderot's theory,[1] which leaves no scope for sentiment and passion, but substitutes tears and sobs for everything else. Nevertheless, in spite of his severe handling of *Phèdre*, it is clear that Fénelon was more sympathetic towards Racine than towards Corneille. He tells us a very interesting fact, and one which is not to be found in Racine's Life by his son, namely, that our great poet had conceived the idea of writing a tragedy without love, after the pattern of the Greeks, the theme of which would have been Orestes. Finally, even the magnificent scene between Cinna and Augustus[2] finds no favour in the sight of our critic. He condemns it on the score of its pomp and bombast, which are alien to antiquity, and he prefers the narrative in Suetonius.

In a word, it may be said that Fénelon has not appraised sufficiently highly the beauties of French tragedy. There is some truth in his criticisms, and perhaps, according to the highest canons of taste, Aeschylus

[1] *Cf.* Note lxviii, p. 287.
[2] *Cf.* Note lxix, p. 287.

and Sophocles may be worthy to rank above
Corneille and Racine. But it would only
have been fair to have said that the Moderns
have excelled the Ancients in the portrayal
and analysis of the passions, and that Corneille is unrivalled in originality and grandeur. It is also surprising that Fénelon
does not allude to the experiment in sacred
tragedy, to which we are indebted for
Esther and *Athalie ;* it is obvious that the
latter play was not yet looked upon as the
masterpiece of French tragedy.[1]

Since Fénelon is severe towards tragedy,
because it is too much concerned with love,
it may be expected that he is still more so
towards comedy, which too frequently de-
generates into licence. He deplores the
coarseness of Aristophanes and Plautus ;
but he excuses Terentius, whose pleasing
and refined genius had so much affinity
with his own. What should be specially
noticed is Fénelon's courage in admiring
Molière, although he still makes certain
reservations which may be deemed too
cavilling. We ought to be thankful to a
priest for having spoken in the following
terms of our great comic playwright : " It

[1] *Cf.* Note lxx, p. 287.

must be admitted that Molière is a great comedy-writer. I have no fear in saying that he had a deeper insight into certain characters than Terentius; he treated a greater variety of subjects, and depicted with bold traits every form of depravity, and every kind of ridicule we see around us. Finally, Molière opened up entirely new paths. *Once again, I think him great.*" It is obvious that such a tribute does Molière the greatest honour; and it is also honourable in a priest[1] not to have scrupled to utter such words. To be sure, at the time Fénelon was speaking, Molière had been dead for forty years. He had already gone down to posterity, and he was referred to as one of the great men of antiquity. None the less, it required a certain freedom of spirit to see in him anything but an histrion, and to say: " Once again, I think him great."

As to Fénelon's strictures, they are interesting. He reproaches Molière for his style: " While his thought is good, his expression is often faulty "; he makes use of " a host of metaphors which border on the nonsensical." What is Fénelon alluding to in these

[1] *Cf.* Note lxxi, p. 287.

severe criticisms? As for us, we are of opinion that Molière writes extremely well, and that he has a wonderful mastery of verse. Boileau[1] inquired of him "where he found his rhymes." Fénelon adds that he prefers his prose to his verse, and that "*l'Avare* is *less badly written* than his poetic plays." Would anyone express himself differently concerning a poor stylist? In our opinion, a study of Molière's style might be undertaken, as seen and judged from Fénelon's point of view : it is no doubt the latter's Attic taste which is not satisfied. Moreover, his judgment becomes all the more authoritative when it is compared with that of La Bruyère,[2] who said in the same vein : "The only thing that Molière lacks is the avoidance of jargon and barbarisms."

Two other charges brought against Molière are easier to understand, coming from the pen of Fénelon. The one is Molière's exaggeration : "He has overdrawn his characters, in order to please the pit." In the second place, "he has invested vice with a gracious aspect, and virtue with an odious

[1] *Cf.* Note lxxii, p. 288.
[2] *Cf.* Note lxxiii, p. 288.

and ridiculous austerity." He was referring
to *Don Juan* and the *Misanthrope*, and was
thus paving the way for Rousseau's celebrated attack.[1] Finally, Fénelon is at one
with Boileau in regretting that Molière
should have fallen so low at times, and
should have imitated the coarse side of
Italian comedy. He would willingly have
said with Boileau :

Dans ce sac ridicule où Scapin s'enveloppe
Je ne reconnais plus l'auteur du *Misanthrope*.[2]

It is true that we shall not recognise the
author of the *Misanthrope* in the scene of
Scapin's sack,[3] but neither is that the place
to look for him ; moreover, because one is
the author of the *Misanthrope*, is one never
again to joke ?

One of the last chapters of the *Lettre à
l'Académie* is devoted to history. It is especially here that Fénelon gives proof of new
and prophetic intuitions, for he reveals beforehand the progress which the art of history was destined to make in our time.[4]

[1] *Cf.* Note lxxiv, p. 288.
[2] *Cf.* Note lxxv, p. 288.
[3] *Cf.* Note lxxvi, p. 288.
[4] *Cf.* Note lxxvii, p. 288.

FÉNELON AS LITERARY CRITIC

The first quality he looks for in the historian is impartiality : " He should be of no particular country or epoch." This is asking a great deal. Is there not, perchance, a middle course between cold indifference, and unjust partiality ? Doubtless, history must not be falsified ; but facts being what they are, is the historian to be forbidden to speak of them with emotion ? Is fervour to be denied to an author who is relating the glories of his country, or pity to him who narrates her misfortunes, or, again, indignation to the one who recounts the crimes of history ? All that is required of him is to avoid excess, and to keep within the bounds of moderation.

What Fénelon desires above all else, and in this he is undoubtedly an innovator, is that the historian should bring to his task a keen sense of life and reality : " I prefer," he says, " a somewhat inaccurate historian, who mutilates names, but who naively reproduces all the details like Froissart, to all the chroniclers of Charlemagne." This preference for Froissart is uncommon in the seventeenth century ; it anticipates the modern fondness for the middle ages, and for colour. After life and movement, Fénelon recommends order and clearness. Our understanding of the facts depends upon the historian's talent for composition. "The historian should embrace and possess the whole of his subject; his vision should cover the entire field, as it were, at one sweep. He must exhibit its unity, and show all the events proceeding, so to speak, from a single cause." He must choose, out of twenty positions, the one in which a fact may be placed to the best advantage, in order to shed light upon all the others. A fact often indicates beforehand, and explains in advance, coming events; on the other hand, it frequently happens that another fact will appear in a better light, if relegated to the background. The style should be simple and devoid of ornaments; the narrative will thus gain in concision, animation, and grace. An affected writer despises an unadorned chronicle; he desires to dress it, and deck it out with embellishments, and, so to speak, give it curls. The good historian, on the contrary, is careful not to add to the nobility and majesty of the bare facts. The majority of the preceding remarks on order, clearness, and simplicity, are eminently applicable to Thiers. His next remarks would almost appear to have a direct reference to Augustin Thierry. For Fénelon requires what he terms "le costume," that is to say, truth of historical colour. He will have the historian respect the manners and customs of the past. Clovis must not be represented in the midst of a polished, gallant, and splendid Court; nor must the French of the time of Henry II be depicted with wigs and cravats, nor again those of the seventeenth century, with beards and ruffs.

Another novelty on the part of Fénelon is the importance which he attaches to the history of the institutions and changes in the government of nations. Here it is not Thierry, but Guizot whom he seems to foresee, and to call up before our mind, when, for instance, he shows us the importance of the Salic lands among the Franks, the difference between the beneficiary earldoms, under Charlemagne, and the hereditary earldoms, under his successors; he asks that the Parliaments of the second race, which were national assemblies, should be distinguished from those of the third race, which were judicial institutions. "We must know," he adds, "the origin of fiefs,

the services of feudatories, the enfranchise-
ment of the serfs, the growth of corporations,
the rise of the Third Estate, the introduction of 'clercs,' and of permanent troops."
Thus, in a few rapid touches, Fénelon sum-
marises the chief events in the internal
history of France, which have been the
subject of such profound and original
investigations in our day.[1]

We have omitted to refer to eloquence,
because Fénelon also dealt with this subject
in a separate work, the *Dialogues sur l'Éloquence*. Despite its reputation, this work
is far from possessing the interest and charm
of the *Lettre à l'Académie*. In the first place,
it must be acknowledged that the dialogue
form, notwithstanding the fine example
set by Plato, is anything but an advantage.
It is long, cold, and monotonous ; there is
hardly an author who has been successful
with it. Fénelon's three interlocutors, A,
B, and C, are lifeless and colourless. C
hardly serves any purpose at all ; B is a
simple soul, whom everything fills with
astonishment. As a matter of fact only A
speaks, and he would be more interesting
if he really stood alone, and if he had

[1] *Cf.* Note lxxviii, p. 288.

condensed all he has to say. An interlocutor is only of service to express a few objections, which an author can just as well address to himself, if he desires. The essence of the teaching, borrowed from Plato, is, however, eminently sound. It amounts to this, that the orator must not speak for the sake of speaking, or please, merely in order to please ; but he must speak and please that he may. persuade, and convince people of truth and righteousness. It is the expansion of the celebrated dictum *vir bonus dicendi peritus*.[1] As to the type of eloquence, Fénelon prefers, as we should expect, spontaneous and rapid oratory to florid and rhetorical oratory. He esteems Demosthenes above Isocrates and Cicero. On this point the *Lettre à l'Académie* is a brilliant and delightful commentary on the theory of the *Dialogues*.

The *Dialogues sur l'Éloquence* are especially interesting and original in their treatment of pulpit oratory. He wages war chiefly against three faults : the first is the abuse of texts ;[2] the second, the abuse of divisions ; the third, the custom of learning

[1] *Cf.* Note lxxix, p. 289.
[2] *Cf.* Note lxxx, p. 289.

sermons and speeches by heart. The first proceeds from faulty taste ; the second, from the abuse of scholastic subtleties ; the third, from a kind of mental laziness, which causes the orator to shrink from facing a subject, and to prefer to arrive in advance fully armed. On this last point Fénelon is particularly strong, insistent, and persuasive. He shows the superiority of extempore speech, even when carefully prepared, over the written discourse : " Consider," he says, " the advantages enjoyed by the man who does not learn by heart. He is in full possession of himself ; he speaks naturally, his thoughts flow spontaneously, his expressions are lively and full of movement, the very warmth that animates him, causes him to find expressions and figures, which he would never have prepared in his study. What the orator lights upon in the heat of action, is far more communicative and direct ; it appears unstudied, and savours of artlessness. Add to this that an able orator accommodates his matter to the impression he finds that it is making on his audience ; he takes up his theme again from a different point of view ; he clothes it in fresh images. You see that the orator, who is speaking from memory, is far from attaining this end.

All this advice is perfectly sound, on condition, however, that we do not understand by this that the orator is to rely entirely upon extemporisation. On the other hand, extemporisation by itself is generally superficial and commonplace. One's soul is not always at a sufficiently high pitch to discover brilliant expressions and powerful effects. Meditation alone supplies profound thoughts and original expressions. Fénelon, then, does not say that the orator is not to prepare his discourse. He even goes so far as to admit that a few glowing passages and striking images may be prepared beforehand. The only essential point in his theory is that the orator should not learn his speech by heart : a reciter is not a speaker. The orator, who recites, becomes a kind of actor, who retails another man's work. Moreover, nothing precludes a man from writing out his speech after it has been delivered, as the Ancients did, in order to endow it with perfect artistic form ; but by so doing he forfeits the right of delivering it again.

We may also endorse what Fénelon says

about the abuse of divisions ; but by this we are to understand those over-subtle divisions which are based upon antitheses ; otherwise, division is in the nature of things, and a discourse without divisions would lack order and clearness.

Such are Fénelon's chief views concerning eloquence ; they are the outcome of the same spirit, and the same preferences which he exhibits in every other department, namely, a love for all that is simple,[1] natural, and unconstrained. But he is not entirely free from over-sanguine confidence, when he attributes to the inspiration of the moment, a power and fruitfulness which it does not always possess.

[1] *Cf*. Note lxxxi, p. 290.

CHAPTER XI

FÉNELON AT CAMBRAI

In the month of August, 1696, Fénelon
was bidden by the King to proceed to the
town of Cambrai, of which he had been
appointed Archbishop, and to await there
Rome's pronouncement on the question of
the *Maximes*. This was an order of exile ;
and from that time forward, Fénelon did
not appear at Court, nor did he even leave
his diocese. What life did he lead there ?
What were his habits, occupations, and
trials ? We are told by a charming writer,
with whose permission we propose to borrow
freely from his interesting study of the
subject.[1]

A few years previously Cambrai had been
added to France by the Treaty of Nime-
guen. It was a rich demesne, with a magnificent Palace ; and the Archbishop of
Cambrai was thus a really great lord. Here
Fénelon succeeded in ordeiing his life with
dignified simplicity.

Bossuet's secretary, Abbé Le Dieu, has

[1] *Fénelon à Cambrai*, by Emmanuel de Broglie, 1884.

left us a picture of a day spent in Fénelon's
company. The details he gives are so exact
and vivid, that we can imagine we are there
too. " The Prelate was in long violet robes,
cassock and simarre with silk facings, and
deep scarlet buttons and buttonholes. His
waist was girt with neither tassel nor gold
fringe, and his hat was ornamented with
a band of green silk ribbon ; he wore white
gloves, but carried neither stick nor cloak.
As dinner had already been announced, he
rose and invited me to come and take a
seat at his table. All the guests were await-
ing him in the dining hall. Hands were
washed without ceremony. The Prelate
blessed the repast, and took the chief seat.
Abbé de Chanterac was on his left ; the
company were seated at random ; the seat
on his right being vacant, he made a sign
to me to come and occupy it. The meal
was served in grand and exquisite style.
The menu comprised several kinds of soup ;
good beef and mutton, all sorts of entrées
and stews, a huge piece of roast meat, par-
tridges, and all manner of game, glorious
fruit, excellent red wine, but no beer, and
delicious bread. The table linen was spot-
lessly clean, and the plate was massive

silver. The Archbishop took the trouble of helping me to the daintiest morsels with his own hand ; I thanked him, hat in hand ; and he never once failed to raise his hat to me in return. The conversation was quite unconstrained, pleasant, and even lively. The Prelate spoke in his turn, and allowed courteous freedom to all. He himself ate very little, and nothing but easily assimilable food ; he drank only two or three draughts of a light white wine of pale colour. It is not surprising that he is exceedingly thin ; he is, nevertheless, in very good health. I think chagrin is wearing him. He looks very mortified. After dinner, the whole company adjourned to the Archbishop's large bedroom. He was seated in front of the fire-place, towards the middle of the room, and had a little writing-table by his side. Coffee was served ; there was enough for everyone present. The conversation turned on the latest news. After supper, I was requested to speak about the death of M. de Meaux. They inquired whether he had been conscious of his approaching end, and whether he had received the sacraments. But the Prelate expressly asked me who prepared him for death. I thought that by putting this last question to me, he wished to signify that at death M. de Meaux needed good advice, and a person of authority, especially after having played a part in so many important and delicate matters ; but, during the whole of this conversation, the Archbishop never uttered a single word in praise of M. de Meaux." This silence on Fénelon's part has been criticised, and it has been taken as a sign of enmity and ill-will. The friends of the Prelate have replied that praise would have savoured of hypocrisy. It seems to me that a middle course might have been found between these two extremes. It is probable that Fénelon, despite his ready wit, failed to find then and there the right thing to say, and that he preferred to remain silent, rather than utter empty words contrary to his convictions.

Besides this description of the outward circumstances of Fénelon's life, as witnessed by a stranger, we have, from Fénelon's own pen, a picture of his inner life, of his weaknesses and mental unrest, perhaps, too, of his regrets and fears. "I hate the world," he writes ; "I despise it, and yet it flatters me a little. I feel the gradual approach of old age, and I am growing accustomed to it without losing my hold on life ; when I examine myself, I seem as though I were in a dream, and I appear to myself like a picture in a vision ; I think I have no desire to taste of the world ; it seems as if there were a barrier between it and me, which prevents any longing on my part, and which would, I fancy, stand not a little in my way, were I one day called upon to return to it. There is a fundamental element of self-interest and instability in me of which I am ashamed. The slightest thing that saddens me makes me dejected, while the smallest matter that pleases me a little, elates me beyond measure. Nothing is so humiliating as to be thus lenient towards oneself, and hard on others, so cowardly at the sight of even the shadow of a cross, and so prone to cast every burden off at the least glimmer of joy. But all is good. God opens a strange book before us for our instruction, when he makes us read our own hearts. I am to myself, as it were, the whole of a great diocese, more burdensome than the outside one, and a diocese which I am incapable of reforming."

Fénelon's only recreation was walking. It served as a pretext for converse with his friends, when he would display the riches of his charming intelligence. "No one," says Saint-Simon, "possessed in a higher degree than he, the happy gift of easy conversation, light, yet always becoming; intercourse with him was enchanting; the ease and even tenour of his piety caused none to be scared; he never aimed at exhibiting more wit than those with whom he was conversing."

Let us now consider him in his episcopal administration. As soon as he was appointed to the Archbishopric of Cambrai in 1694, Fénelon undertook, contrary to the custom of a great number of Prelates of the time, to spend nine months of the year in his diocese. Exile, therefore, did not make much difference to his plans: it meant three months more residence, and absence from Court. His chief difficulty was to gain the good will of the people. Cambrai had only recently been added to the Crown. The inhabitants were Flemish, and very much opposed, by their language, manners, and customs, to the French spirit. A large portion of the diocese which was under Fénelon's spiritual jurisdiction, was still under the domination of the Empire; he had thus to rule over a foreign, and almost hostile, country. His difficulties were greatly increased during the war which for several years brought France and the Empire to grips, and which was waged chiefly in the Flemish provinces. We can imagine what efforts Fénelon had to put forth, in order to ingratiate himself with the inhabitants of these parts. His marvellous gift of pleasing, and his resourceful dexterity, had to reveal themselves in all manner of directions, and in time they succeeded in winning the hearts of the people. Writing to the Duke of Beauvillier, he describes the happy result of his conduct, in the following words: "I proceed cautiously, and humour their minds, in order that I may place myself in a position to be of service to them; they are fairly fond of me, because they find that I am not haughty, but quiet and uniform in my demeanour. They have discovered that I am neither unyielding, nor interested, nor sly; they trust me readily enough; and our good Flemings, however clumsy they may appear, are more cunning than I care to be."

A great part of his time at Cambrai was taken up by the controversy with the Jansenists. One is surprised to find that a

theologian, who had himself just been denounced in Rome as tainted with heresy, and
who had seen the danger of a too narrow
orthodoxy, should have spoken out with such
force against a doctrine which had enlisted
so many great minds on its side. It would
seem, too, that an Archbishop, who had
been condemned by the Pope, could not
have much authority to determine the rela-
tive proportions of truth and error, in the
conflict which Jansenism had raised in the
bosom of the Church. Some have thought
to discover the motive for Fénelon's severity
towards the Jansenists, in the fact of his
own condemnation. He desired, so they
say, to curry favour with the King and the
Church, and to cause them to forget his
own errors. This is possible, and it was
undoubtedly a regrettable thing for a leader
of the Church to have called down upon his
own head the censure of the highest Catholic
authority. Yet, the fact of his having erred
was surely not a reason for him to renounce
his archiepiscopal prerogatives, and become
the accomplice of every form of error. Fénelon had always been opposed to Jansenism.
He could not belie his own opinions when
once he was at the head of a diocese, where

it was more than ever his bounden duty to uphold the faith. Moreover, Fénelon was drawn into this controversy, not on account of any purely theoretical and doctrinal zeal, but because of the exigencies of his episcopal administration. Flanders, which was under his spiritual authority, was filled with Jansenists, and was, indeed, the chief centre of their theological propaganda.[1] As Archbishop, Fénelon could not remain indifferent to their enterprises. He must either combat them, or else resign his functions, a thing he had no reason to do. It appears to us, therefore, that the ardour displayed by Fénelon throughout this controversy, did not exceed what was not only his right, but even his duty.

Besides, although Fénelon showed himself, both dogmatically and dialectically, severe towards the doctrines of Jansenism, he exhibited, in practice, great kindliness and real tolerance towards individual Jansenists. Saint-Simon, who was, as we know, but little predisposed in his favour, says : " Fénelon was always consistent in his conduct. The Low Countries swarmed with Jansenists, or people regarded as such. His

[1] *Cf.* Note lxxxii, p. 290.

diocese in particular, and Cambrai itself, were filled with them. Both were constant places of refuge and peace for them. Happy and content to find a quiet asylum there, they took no notice of their Archbishop who, albeit inimical to their doctrine, allowed them entire freedom. They relied on others for their dogmatic defence, and did little to impair the universal love which all felt for Fénelon." [1]

The same tolerance was extended to the Protestants. Fénelon was opposed to measures of violence : " The public rumour in these parts is that the Council takes none but rigorous measures, in its dealings with the Huguenots. *This is not the true spirit of the Gospel.*" He gave evidence of this tolerance on several occasions, and on the following, amongst others : certain peasants, close to the frontier, passed for recent converts, and outwardly adhered to the Catholic forms of worship ; then they crossed the frontier, in order to take part in the ceremonies of their former faith. Fénelon, although grieved at this sacrilegious profanation, obtained passports to enable them to leave the country, a great

[1] *Cf.* Note lxxxiii, p. 290.

favour in those days, for people were then rigorously forbidden to quit the territory.

Another important aspect of Fénelon's life at Cambrai, was his noble and generous conduct during the war. The following, according to Emmanuel de Broglie, are the outstanding features of this period : " When, in 1708, owing to our defeats, the war was carried forward into the districts surrounding Cambrai, Fénelon's charity grew with the needs of the people, and his benefactions became more numerous. The country clergy, relying on the tithe for their living, were entirely ruined, and unable to supply the State with the extraordinary contributions levied for war purposes. Fénelon made himself responsible for this tax, and paid it out of his own pocket. The following year, after Malplaquet, Cambrai was filled with pilgrims and fugitives, who came in crowds to seek a refuge for themselves and their flocks. Fénelon opened wide the doors of his Palace ; every corner was occupied. The courtyards and gardens were full of cattle and horned animals, rescued from the pillage of the foreign troops. Fénelon provided for this colony at his own expense, saying : ' God will help us.' Next came the turn of the wounded officers and soldiers. Fénelon again threw open his house ; he had 150 persons at his table. He ordered his Seminary to be evacuated, and had the wounded placed there, and tended at his own expense. At the same time, he furnished the French troops with corn, and thus saved them from dying of hunger, after the terrible winter of 1709. Even his enemies did not escape his bounty : ' He won the affection of the enemy,' says Saint-Simon, ' because of his care for those who were detained as prisoners at Cambrai, even accommodating under his own roof the officers of the enemy, and showering his gifts upon their soldiers equally with our own ; so much so, that the leaders of their troops, Prince Eugene and the Duke of Marlborough, gave him constant proofs of their consideration in every way, even to the point of abstaining from foraging in his fields, and sparing those which he asked them to respect.' Hence, the lands of the Archbishop of Cambrai became places of refuge for the peasants ; and these well-cultivated fields provided corn in abundance, which Fénelon placed at the disposal of the army, and the value of which was never refunded. ' It is incredible,' says

FÉNELON AT CAMBRAI

Saint-Simon, ' to what a height his name and reputation were carried by this conduct. The King, who could not remain in ignorance of it, and who took umbrage at such applause, and Mme de Maintenon still more, could not refrain from letting him know on several occasions that he was grateful to him for the succour he afforded to his troops.' "

The most important event which marked the last years of Fénelon's life was, first, the sudden advent of his pupil, the Duke of Burgundy, to the position of Dauphin, and then, after six months, the death of this Prince, with whom vanished all Fénelon's hopes for his country, and perhaps also for himself. The death of His Royal Highness, so dramatically narrated by Saint-Simon, had put an end to the subordinate and timorous part played by the Duke of Burgundy. He had become the idol of the Court. Louis XIV had admitted him to a share in the government. The little coterie of the Dukes of Beauvillier and Chevreuse, which had been so long under a cloud, and menaced because of its fidelity to Fénelon, now became the centre round' which the courtiers revolved. Fénelon, in Cambrai, felt the effects of the general bewitchment. People knew the influence he would wield under the future King; popular favour, therefore, returned to him. Everything passed through Cambrai. Fénelon continued to correspond with the young Prince, and to offer him the advice which his youth demanded. Then meetings were held to draw up plans of government; we have already given a summary of what is known as the *Tables de Chaulnes*.[1] All was in readiness for a new reign, fresh, brilliant, and liberal, and one wherein patriotism, peace, and virtue would be enthroned. Then a terrible blow fell, and all these hopes were overthrown. The Duchess of Burgundy died after a short illness, and a few days later, the turn of the Duke of Burgundy came: struck down by an unknown malady, and having apparently lost the soul of his life, he died on February 16th, 1712, not without some appearances of having been poisoned, a suspicion which Fénelon himself did not entirely dismiss. What a sudden change of fortune! What a mysterious revolution, coming unexpectedly to substitute the reign of vice for that of virtue, the Regent for

[1] *Cf.* pp. 175–6, *supra.*

the Duke of Burgundy! What a blow for Fénelon especially, he who had already been so cruelly hit by exile and persecution, and before whom an unexpected ray of light appeared for a moment to have opened up again a highway to the Court and to fortune! What a struggle in his soul between the last irrepressible regrets of a profane and lawful ambition, and the humble and sublime submission of Christian piety! Now at last, he experienced the vanity of human vanities, the overthrow of defeated illusions, the sorrows of an old age without hope, change, or pleasure. That love of God, for which he had suffered so many things, must undoubtedly have consoled him, and renewed his courage under such sad circumstances. Who would imagine that it was after these painful trials, and only a few months before his death, that Fénelon wrote that beautiful *Lettre à l'Académie Française*, so lively and florid, so replete with pagan reminiscences, and so worldly and charming in tone? Literature is the great consoler, in another sense, but no less sweetly than religion.

Fénelon survived his pupil only a few years. Sorrow, heavy work, and a delicate constitution had undermined his health. An unfortunate occurrence produced a fatal shock to the system. During one of his episcopal rounds, his carriage was overturned,[1] No one was injured ; but, says Saint-Simon, " he realised the danger to the full, and his weak frame bore the entire brunt of the accident. He felt indisposed on his arrival at Cambrai. Fever set in, and Fénelon perceived that his hour had come. Either because of his disgust with a world, which had so constantly deceived him, and with its passing show, or because of his genuine piety, strengthened by long practice, he appeared to be indifferent to all he was leaving, and entirely absorbed in what he was going to meet, in a state of tranquillity and peace, which did not banish all anxiety, while leaving ample room for penitence, mental detachment, and exclusive attention to spiritual concerns, and finally, a trust which rose triumphant over fear and humility."

Fénelon fell ill on the first day of January, 1715 ; he died on the seventh, eight months before Louis XIV. An eye-witness has left us a touching record of his death. The account is too lengthy to be reproduced in

[1] *Cf.* Note lxxxiv, p. 292.

its entirety ; we will merely give a few extracts as reported in Cardinal de Bausset's *Histoire de Fénelon.*[1]

" This illness, which lasted only six days, and was accompanied by very acute pain, was an unintermittent fever, the cause of which was hidden. During the whole of these six days, he refused all entertainment, save the reading of the Holy Scriptures. For the first few days, they deferred to his wishes at intervals only, fearing lest the sedulous care with which he followed this reading should prevent the medicine from taking effect, and should irritate his complaint. At first they read to him only from the Book of Tobit ; then they added little by little, and as occasion required, a few passages on the fragility of temporal goods, and on the hope of everlasting possessions.

" He had himself carried from the little room, which he usually occupied, into the large one. He desired that all the members of his Chapter should be able to enter, and be present at the religious ceremony preceding the reception of the viaticum ; he addressed a few words of edification to the entire company, words which I was unable

[1] Vol. iv, bk. 8, p. 376.

to hear, being at too great a distance from
his bed.

"In the course of the afternoon of the
fourth day of his illness, his nephews, Abbé
de Beaumont and the Marquis of Fénelon,
arrived post from Paris; their presence
greatly consoled him; he inquired who had
given them the alarm; grief prevented their
uttering a single word; all they could do
was to point to Abbé de Fénelon, who was
at Cambrai when the illness declared itself.
. . . They had taken the precaution of
bringing with them the celebrated Chirac,
who held an immediate consultation with
the local doctors; they agreed to bleed him
a second time, and to administer an emetic;
the effect was rapid, and he appeared to
be relieved at once; but it was soon recognised that the complaint was stronger than
any remedy.

"He suffered much during the remainder
of the day, and throughout the last night;
but he rejoiced in that he resembled Christ
in his sufferings. . . . Now and again the
fever would greatly increase, provoking a
state of delirium which vexed him sorely,
although he never uttered a strong or
indecorous word. Immediately upon the

cessation of the paroxysm, he was seen to join his hands together, raise his eyes to heaven, submit himself with resignation, and commune with God, in perfect peace.

" I am still affected when I think of the touching scene of this last night. All the members of his pious family, who were assembled at Cambrai, came one after the other, during the intervals of full consciousness, to ask and receive his blessing. Several other persons from the town likewise presented themselves ; his servants came next, in a body, weeping bitterly. Abbé Le Vayer also received his blessing on behalf of the Seminary and diocese. Abbé Le Vayer then repeated the prayers for the dying, interspersing them with short and touching words from the Scriptures. . . . He passed away peacefully at half-past five in the morning, on the 7th of January, 1715.

" We believe our saintly and pious Archbishop died holily, as he had lived. . . . No ready money was found in his house ; the losses and heavy expenses incurred by the proximity of armies, during the three last campaigns, had completely exhausted his revenues, without his having, even in the slightest degree, cut down the alms

which he was in the habit of giving to the
Convents of the town, to the ordinary poor
of the diocese, to the Sisters of Charity for
the sick poor, to the parishes he visited, to
the students in his diocese, and to a multitude of other people. He left nothing to his
family of the value of his furniture, or
of the arrears due to him from his
farmers. . . ."

Fénelon's death created a profound sensation throughout Europe, where his virtues and genius were admired even more
than in France. We do not know what
impression his death produced on Louis XIV.
The saying attributed to him : " We shall
miss him much upon occasion," does not
appear to rest upon well-authenticated testimony. Mme. de Maintenon refers to him,
in a letter to Mme. de Caylus, in words which
strike me as very cold : " I am sorry for
the death of M. de Cambrai ; he was a friend
of whom I was deprived by Quietism ; but
they say he might have been of service in
the Council, should the latter ever come to
be held." Perhaps Louis XIV's remark, if it
be true, was an allusion to the latter event-
uality. What is certain is that, with his
death, there disappeared a great light, which

might have continued to shine for many years, for Fénelon was then only sixty-four. Saint-Simon inclines to the belief that the Duke of Orleans would have called him to the highest offices of the State. What could Fénelon have done at the Court of the Regent ? He would, in all probability, have declined to take part in the business of the State ; and we have no cause to regret that he was not called upon to re-enter society, a thing which would have been out of keeping both with his years, and with his piety.

Referring to Fénelon's chances of returning to society and power, Saint-Simon speaks of him in rather harsh terms : " It was owing to this oracular authority, which he had acquired over his friends, that he had grown accustomed to a domination which, beneath its apparent gentleness, brooked no resistance. So he would have tolerated no associates had he returned to Court, and entered the Council ; when firmly anchored, and able to dispense with the help of others, it would have proved a very perilous thing to have resisted him, nay more, not to have shown oneself at all times tractable, and filled with admiration for him." [1] Thus, in

[1] Cf. Mémoires, xi, p. 439.

spite of the gentle and seductive sides of his nature, there may have co-existed I know not what elements of sternness and imperiousness, which would have made themselves felt, had he been raised to a position of power.

We catch glimpses of these aspects of his character in his letters to the Duke of Burgundy. A Sovereign would not have found him a counsellor easy to deal with. Courtiers would have hated him. An enemy of despotism, he himself would perhaps have shown himself a benevolent despot. But we are not called upon to judge what did not take place, and Fénelon, unfortunately or fortunately, missed this opportunity of enhancing his name, or avoided the risk of tarnishing it.

Notwithstanding the severity which Saint-Simon exhibits towards Fénelon, he is, nevertheless, the most favourable witness we possess, and the one who has left us the noblest picture of this great man. Concerning his life and residence at Cambrai, he writes thus : " His alms, his episcopal visitations, repeated several times a year, the wisdom and benignity of his government, his frequent preaching in towns and villages, his easy access, his humanity towards the poor, his courtesy to all classes, the natural grace which enhanced the value of everything he said and did—all these things caused him to be adored by the people ; and his clergy, whom he called sons and brothers, enthroned him in their hearts. Amid all this eager and universal desire to please, there was nothing mean or ordinary, affected or out of place ; there was never any scandal or violence against anyone ; everything about and around him was in the most perfect order." [1] What more could Fénelon's most ardent admirers require ! If this was the language of an enemy, what must that of his friends have been ?

In conclusion, let us recall a few of the principal traits which characterise the personality of Fénelon, as we have tried to describe it in these pages. In our opinion, what stands out above every other quality is his broad-mindedness, and especially the fact of its existence in a believing soul, in which it would seem that no element of modern doubt, or of the unrest of free thought, ever penetrated. As truly attached to the faith as any Christian of his day (save as

[1] *Cf. Mémoires,* xi, p. 441.

regards a few debatable points of high theology), he found it possible to combine, with
perfect ease, scrupulous obedience to authority, with a strong and extensive relish for
novelty ; he anticipated the needs of the
modern mind ; on certain essential matters,
he thought as we do ; he is one of our con-
temporaries. The eighteenth century endeavoured to claim him, but he was of too
refined a nature for so violent and unpolished
an age ; he has more affinity with our
own, which is the century of nice distinctions,
the balancing of opinions, bold innovation
tempered by equity, and a clear understanding of all things. Fénelon too is discriminating and conscientious ; his is a
really free and open mind. In all things,
he is in favour of the liberal, or, as we should
term it to-day, the advanced solution. In
literature, he surpassed Boileau ; in theology
and philosophy, Bossuet ; in politics, Riche-
lieu and Louis XIV. He was in favour of
the better instruction of women, of new
departures in literature, of Descartes'
methodical doubt, and of the sovereignty
of the nation ; in theology and philosophy,
he reached the highest peaks of refinement
and sublimity. He dared to place the most

unpalatable truths before Kings ; and, in particular, he wrote to the King of France the most extraordinary letter that has ever been seen :[1] on this occasion, however, his true genius failed him, for violence and unbecoming harshness for once took the place of his habitual moderation and delicacy of touch ; this time, but this time only, the liberal was merged in the revolutionist.

We are justified in saying that, as a man, Fénelon was one of the most complex of characters. He was loved and respected by the greatest people of his time ; he was also attacked by the greatest. Mme. de Maintenon said : " I know of no one who can compare with M. de Cambrai for candour." And Bossuet accused him of duplicity and hypocrisy ; let us discount from this judgment all that is inspired by the passions of combat ; there still remains more suppleness and ingenuity than it behoves a saint or an angel to possess. Fénelon was neither an angel nor a saint. He was a man. He was ambitious, as he had a right to be. He defended himself with boldness and temerity, as well as with skill, and at times perhaps with cunning. But all this is covered by

[1] *Cf.* Note lxxxv, p. 292.

the splendour of his exile, and by his noble
life as an Archbishop. Greatness and nobility
are the distinguishing characteristics of his
life. The legends which have gathered round
the name of Fénelon are, at bottom, as true
as all legends : he remains the most fascinating and enchanting personage of the
seventeenth century. It would be an injustice to his memory to seek to efface and
destroy this aspect of the classical Fénelon,
on behalf of a conventional Fénelon, the
principal features of whose personality are
furnished by Saint-Simon. In order not to
be misled in our judgments on great men,
we must make certain allowances for the
malignity of their enemies ; but that were
a sorry philosophy, as Rousseau said, which
should force us " to discredit Socrates, and
defame Regulus."

NOTES

Note I, to p. 10.   Mazarin's death, in 1661, was the signal for a recrudescence of intolerant methods towards the Protestants.   Louis XIV's relentless policy of suppression of the political liberties enjoyed by the Huguenots since Henri IV's Edict of 1598, and his efforts to crush out religious dissent, took two forms principally : on the one hand, allurements to the wavering in the shape of privileges and exemptions promised to the " converted," and, on the other hand, persecution of the recalcitrants.   The merciless application of physical force began in 1661, with the sending of soldiers, especially Dragoons (whence the name of Dragonnades given to these *missions bottées*), to the provinces of Poitou first, (under the brutal and sanguinary Intendant Marillac), then Saintonge, Limousin, Guyenne, Languedoc, and Bearn.   The two chief results were : the forced abjuration of several thousands of Protestants, and the ruinous emigration of more than a quarter of a million Huguenots to England, America, Holland, Switzerland, and other reformed countries.

Writing on October 28th, 1685, a week after the Revocation of the Edict of Nantes, and referring to Father Bourdaloue, one of the missionaries, who, like Fénelon, had been sent in the wake of the armies to " confirm " the newly " converted," Mme. de Sévigné says : " Il s'en va, par ordre du Roi, prêcher à Montpellier, et dans ces provinces où tant de gens se sont convertis sans savoir pourquoi.   Le P. Bourdaloue le leur apprendra et en fera de bons Catholiques.   Les Dragons out été de très bons missionnaires jusqu'ici : les prédicateurs qu'on envoie présentement rendront l'ouvrage parfait."   The irony of the words " sans savoir pourquoi," is paralleled by the following, in a letter written by Fénelon to Bossuet : " Si l'on veut leur faire abjurer le Christianisme et adopter le Coran, il n'y a qu' à leur renvoyer les Dragons."

It is related of Fénelon that, upon one occasion, after having driven a cow to an old Huguenot woman, who had been looking for it for some time, the young missioner entered into conversation with her in the hope of converting her. The old woman held her ground firmly, and, at length, Fénelon having asked her : " Where was your Church two hundred years ago ? " —she replied : " In hearts like yours ! "

Cf. Élie Benoît *Histoire de l'Édit de Nantes* (1693-95), and Jules Michelet, *Louis XIV et la Révocation de l'Édit de Nantes*, one of the twenty-eight vols. of his *Histoire de France* (not entirely impartial, especially as regards the religious affairs of the reign of Louis XIV).

Note II, to p. 10.—Toleration, one of the least conspicuous of the Christian virtues, in spite of the best minds in the Church since Saint Justin the Martyr, Origen, and Saint Hilary of Poitiers, is the subject of an excellent Treatise by Voltaire, written in 1763, in connection with the rehabilitation of the murdered Protestant Jean Calas. Voltaire also wrote an eloquent and passionate plea in his article *Tolérance*, in the *Dictionnaire Philosophique* (1764). The other most important advocates of religious liberty are Bayle, in his *Dictionnaire historique et critique*, and J. J. Rousseau, in his *Contrat social*, Bk. IV, ch. 8 (De la religion civile), and in the *Lettres de la Montagne*, Pt. I, Letter 1.

Lecky gives a summary history of Toleration in France, in the chapter on Persecution in his *History of the Rise and Influence of the Spirit of Rationalism in Europe*, Vol. II, pp. 57-70. *Cf.* also Pierre Lanfrey, *L'Église et les Philosophes au XVIIIᵉ siècle* (1855), and John Morley, *Voltaire*, ch. V.

NOTES

In the following paragraph of his beautiful *Éloge* de Fénelon, crowned by the French Academy in 1771, D'Alembert bears witness to Fénelon's essentially tolerant spirit : " Pendant la guerre de 1701, un jeune Prince de l'armée des alliés passa quelque temps à Cambrai. Fénelon donna quelques instructions à ce Prince, qui l'écoutait avec vénération et avec tendresse. Il lui recommanda surtout de *ne jamais forcer ses sujets à changer de religion*. Nulle puissance humaine, lui disait-il, n'a droit sur la liberté du cœur. *La violence ne persuade pas ; elle ne fait que des hypocrites.* Donner de tels prosélytes à la religion, ce n'est pas la protéger, c'est la mettre en servitude."

But Fénelon was fifty when these words were uttered, and it is probable that any youthful illusions he may have had, regarding the moral lawfulness and value of inquisitorial methods, had by then been shattered by the knowledge that too many so-called conversions had in reality been nothing but hypocritical surrenders, and by the shame-inspiring memory of the inward victories and unflinching faith of those Huguenots, who had endured nameless tortures rather than accept the deliverance placed before them, and who were worthy to rank by the side of the heroes described in Hebrews XI, 35-38 ! Have we not the example of Bishop Fléchier, who had himself been one of these missioners in Brittany, and who lived long enough to proclaim : " Nous savons que la foi se persuade et ne se commande point ! "

Note III, to p. 10.—Marie-Joseph Chénier (1764-1811), brother of the unfortunate lyric poet André Chénier, was the most applauded dramatist of the Revolutionary period. One of the *habitués* of Mme. de Staël's Salon, in 1795, with Daunou, Cabanis, and Benjamin Constant, this noble-minded, but inferior poet, and pupil of Voltaire, " attacha à Melpomène la cocarde

FÉNELON

nationale," according to Camille Desmoulins' dictum. His five act tragedy *Fénelon, ou les Religieuses de Cambrai*, was produced at the Théâtre de la République (Théâtre Français), in February, 1793, less than three weeks after the execution of Louis XVI. The play was a great success, and powerfully contributed to the propagation of what is termed the *légende de Fénelon*. The subject of this tragedy, which is of the same lineage as Diderot's novel *La Religieuse* (1775), is founded on an anecdote attributed to Fléchier, Bishop of Nîmes, and related by D'Alembert. In his Preface, Chénier expresses his lofty intention, in the following words : " J'ai cru qu'en nos jours mêlés de sombres orages, lorsque les mauvais citoyens prêchent impunément le brigandage et l'assassinat, il était plus que temps de faire entendre au théâtre cette voix de l'humanité qui retentit toujours dans le cœur des hommes rassemblés."

Note IV, to p. 11.—La Harpe (1739-1803), the critic and writer, whose best work is contained in his voluminous *Lycée*, or *Cours de littérature*, wrote his *Éloge* in 1771 ; it is an admirable and glowing tribute to Fénelon, whom La Harpe always appraised with justice and discrimination.

Note V, to p. 11.—This is the Prelate who was Chaplain to Napoleon the First, and subsequently Bishop of Troyes, and Archbishop of Vienne. *Cf. Correspondance de Fénelon*, IX, p. 216, for a reference to *la Prétendue Tolérance de Fénelon*.

Note VI, to p. 11.—O. Douen (1830——), Protestant pastor, writer, and member of the Société d'Histoire du Protestantisme ; his *Intolérance de Fénelon, études historiques*, appeared in 1872 (second edition, 1875).

Note VII, to p. 11.—Eugène Despois (1818-1876), the distinguished and high-minded author, translator, and editor (with Paul Mesnard) of the works of Molière, in the collection des Grands Ecrivains de la France.

NOTES

Note VIII, to p. **11.**—Orentin Douen maintained his thesis in a book entitled *l'Intolérance de Fénelon*. Eugène Despois replied in an article of the *Revue bleue* of January 9th, 1875, which Douen answered in an article in the same Review, dated October 28th, 1876. As to the letters from Saintonge, a very unfaithful edition of them was published by Abbé Verlaque ; L. Gazier, in an article of the *Revue bleue* of January 9th, 1875, pointed out the numerous inaccuracies of this edition, and drew special attention to the omission of the whole of one letter, which, it must be admitted, reflects most discreditably on Fénelon. It is nothing short of a recommendation to the Minister Seignelay to bribe a Dutch pamphleteer, Aubert de Versé, to write against Jurieu. [Note by Janet.]

Note IX, to p. **13.**—Concerning all these letters, as well as others, Douen's article in the *Revue bleue* of October 28th, 1876, and also the one by Gazier referred to above, should be consulted. Each letter should, however, be discussed separately. For example, as regards the drawing of corpses on a hurdle, Fénelon declares that " the impression produced is regrettable, that it encourages hypocrisy, that it were preferable to resort to a little patience," etc. Are these expressions of approbation or of disapproval ? [Note by Janet.]

Note X, to p. **19.**—The charming edition given by Octave Gréard, in the *Librairie des bibliophiles*, should be referred to. It is accompanied by a most exquisite and exhaustive Introduction, which leaves nothing more to be said on the subject. His masterly *Éducation des femmes par les femmes* (1886) is also indispensable. *Cf.* Paul Rousselot, *Histoire de l'Éducation des femmes en France* (1883), and Jules Bertaut, *La jeune fille dans la littérature française* (1911).

Note XI, to p. **20.**—This is part of Chrysale's last speech, in Act II, scene 7, of Molière's *Femmes Savantes*.

FÉNELON

Note XII, to p. 23.—*Cf.* J. J. Rousseau, *Émile*, Book I, (first half), and John Morley's *Rousseau*, II, ch. 4, p. 248.

Note XIII, to p. 25.—Fénelon's remarkable Treatise on the " Education of Girls " was written in 1681, when he was only thirty. It is interesting to compare his thoughts with the following " pedagogical " plays of Molière : *Les Précieuses Ridicules* (1659), *L'École des Femmes* (1662), *La Critique de l'École des Femmes* (1663), and *Les Femmes Savantes* (1672).

Note XIV, to p. 28.—Montaigne, in the twenty-fifth chapter of the First Book of his *Essais*, has left us an admirable little Treatise on " The Institution and Education of Children." Like J. J. Rousseau later, in the *Émile*, Montaigne advises the teacher to avoid the fatal mistake of making knowledge and virtue wear a forbidding aspect of difficulty and austerity. His ideal of the *utile dulci* is well expressed in the following passage, remarkable both for its wisdom and its eloquence : " La vertu n'est pas, comme dit l'école, plantée à la tête d'un mont coupé, raboteux, et inaccessible ; ceux qui l'ont approchée la tiennent, au rebours, logée dans une belle plaine fertile et fleurissante, d'où elle voit bien sous soi toutes choses ; mais si peut on y arriver qui en sait l'addresse, par des routes ombrageuses, gazonnées, et doux-fleurantes, plaisamment et d'une pente facile et polie comme est celle des voûtes célestes. Pour n'avoir hanté cette vertu, belle, triomphante, amoureuse, délicieuse pareillement et courageuse, ennemie professe et irréconciliable d'aigreur, de déplaisir, de crainte et de contrainte, ayant pour guide nature, fortune et volupté pour compagnes, ils sont allés, selon leur faiblesse, feindre cette sotte image, triste, querelleuse, dépite, menaceuse, mineuse, et la placer sur un rocher à l'écart, emmi des ronces : fantôme à étonner les gens. . . . Le prix et hauteur de la vraie vertu est en la facilité, utilité et plaisir de son exercice ; si éloigné de difficulté que les enfants y peuvent comme les hommes, les simples comme les subtils. Le règlement, c'est son outil, non pas la force. Socrates, son premier mignon, quitte à escient sa force, pour glisser en la naïveté et aisance de son progrès. C'est la mère nourrice des plaisirs humains."

But, in view of the tendency of some modern educationists to make the learner's task *too* easy and pleasant, and to sacrifice discipline, and personal effort on the part of the pupil, Professor Raymond Thamin is well advised in entering a warning against too extreme a reaction against Spartan methods of overseverity : " Cette confusion du jeu et du travail risque de faire perdre au travail son caractère propre et sa valeur morale. Il n'est pas bon que l'effort soit supprimé de l'éducation. Cette réaction contre la méthode d'autorité, justifiée au temps de Fénelon, risque d'aller jusqu'au relâchement de toute discipline. Prendre l'enfant par les sentiments, c'est donner trop de place dans l'éducation à l'habileté individuelle, et faire reposer la moralité de l'enfant sur cette base fragile : une personne humaine. Il peut en résulter dans les rapports du maître et de l'élève un manque de sincérité, le maître faisant de l'affection un moyen d'action, et peut-être aussi l'élève." (*Cf.* Petit de Julleville's *Histoire de la Langue et de la Littérature française*, V, 8, p. 448.)

Note XV, to p. 30.—*Surmenage*, i.e., overwork, a too intense or too prolonged mental effort. The noun is rarely used except in the expression *surmenage intellectuel*. The verb *surmener* is mainly employed in connection with the over-driving of draught animals, the over-riding of saddle horses, and, figuratively, with the sweating of paid labour.

Note XVI, to p. 31.—Although Fénelon is a forerunner as regards many of the most advanced pedagogical notions, he is not the original exponent of object, or nature lessons. This excellent method of concrete teaching is explicitly preconised, long before its modern revival at the hands of Rousseau, Pestalozzi, Froebel, and Mme. Montessori, by Rabelais, in the First Book of his *Gargantua*. In the twenty-third chapter, we are shown the discipline which is applied by the wise preceptor Ponocrates, in the instruction of the youthful Gargantua : " Il s'instruit par la vue des choses autant que par les livres. Il apprend l'astronomie en considérant l'état du ciel, l'histoire naturelle en discourant à table sur l'origine des aliments, la botanique en herborisant ; et quand l'air est pluvieux, au lieu de s'endormir sur ses livres, il visite les ateliers des orfèvres, monnayeurs, tisseurs, imprimeurs, horlogers, apprenant et considérant l'industrie et invention des métiers.". . . " Quant à la connaissance des faits de nature, je veux que tu t'y adonnes consciencieusement, qu'il n'y ait mer, rivière, ni fontaine dont tu ne connaisses les poissons ; tous les oiseaux de l'air, tous les arbres, arbustes, et frutices des forêts, toutes les herbes de la terre, tous les métaux cachés au ventre des abîmes. . . ." " Certes il faut lire les livres des savants ; mais il faut recourir sans cesse à l'expérience." *Cf.* René Millet, *Rabelais*, Ch. IV, p. 170 *et seq.*

Note XVII, to p. 36.—Whether Fénelon was correct or not in ascribing this unenviable superiority to the French nation, even in the seventeenth century, it is beyond doubt that feminine subservience to the tyranny of fashion, however ugly or immodest, and the passion for luxury, sensationalism, and change, which prevail in twentieth century England and America, are at least as pronounced as in France. The well-to-do classes have now no monopoly of the demoralising craze for excessive finery and pleasure. Nor do we need the testimony of a Marie Corelli, in " Free Opinions," a Ouida, in " Critical Studies," or

NOTES

a Crosland, in " Lovely Woman," to convince us of a fact which ought to be, and often is, deplored and denounced by many a so-called ' gloomy ' preacher in all countries,

" Where wealth accumulates, and men decay."

Note XVIII, to p. 51.—Abbé Claude Fleury (1640-1723), an ecclesiastical and pedagogical writer, one of the noblest, simplest, and most disinterested of men. He was associated with Fénelon in the missions of Saintonge and Poitou, in 1685. He spent sixteen years at Court, as sub-tutor to the Dukes of Burgundy, Anjou, and Berri. From 1716 to 1722, he was Confessor to Louis XV.

The best of his numerous works is his *Histoire ecclésiastique* (1691-1722), in twenty volumes. He devoted thirty years to this learned and edifying History, which ends with the Council of Constance in 1414, and which Voltaire has praised as " la meilleure histoire de l'Église qu'on ait jamais faite." He also wrote *Discours sur les libertés de l'Église Gallicane*, and *Traité du choix et de la méthode des Études*. In 1696, he succeeded La Bruyère in the French Academy ; *cf.* D'Alembert's *Éloge* (1782).

Note XIX, to p. 52.—Besides this excellent and trustworthy work, the exact title of which is *Essai de l'histoire monastique de l'Orient* (1678), Louis Bulteau (1625-1693), who was secretary to Louis XIV during his minority, wrote an *Abrégé de l'histoire de l'Ordre de Saint Benoît et des moines d'Occident* (1684).

Note XX, to p. 52.—Géraud de Cordemoy (1620-1684) devoted the last eighteen years of his life to the preparation of a history of Charlemagne. He had undertaken this work, at the request of Bossuet, for the instruction of the Dauphin, to whom he had been appointed Reader. His son, Louis de Cordemoy (1651-1722), continued and edited the work, under the title of *Histoire de France depuis le temps des Gaulois et le*

FÉNELON

commencement de la monarchie jusqu'en 787, (1685-1689) ; it is a useful and erudite compilation.

Note XXI, to p. 57.—Fénelon, who said : " Il faut mériter la louange et la fuir," never fell into the error, so frequent in weak and ignoble souls, of trying to compass worthy ends by the aid of base means ; he never attempted to influence his pupil for good, by pandering to his pride, his vanity, or his caprice. If even merited praise is to be shunned, how much more is mere flattery to be deprecated ! Fénelon insists on the ethics of true praise in the following words : " Les bonnes louanges sont celles que vous me donnerez en mon absence, si je suis assez heureux pour en mériter. Si vous me croyez véritablement bon, vous devez croire aussi que je veux être modeste et craindre la vanité : épargnez-moi donc, si vous m'estimez, et ne me louez pas comme un homme amoureux des louanges." (*Cf. Télémaque*, Book XVI.)

Note XXII, to p. 59.—L. Crouslé says of the *Dialogues* as a whole, that they are a kind of Anti-Machiavelli ; *cf.* his " *Fénelon et Bossuet* " (1894).

Note XXIII, to p. 60.—Fénelon is also far ahead of his time in the matter of Peace :—" Tout le genre humain n'est qu'une famille dispersée sur la face de toute la terre, tous les peuples sont frères et doivent s'aimer comme tels."—" Les hommes sont tous frères, et ils s'entre-déchirent ! Les bêtes farouches sont moins cruelles qu'eux. Les lions ne font point la guerre aux lions, ni les tigres aux tigres ; ils n'attaquent que les animaux d'espèce différente. L'homme seul, malgré sa raison, fait ce que les animaux sans raison ne firent jamais."—" Le besoin de veiller à notre sûreté ne nous donne jamais un titre de prendre la terre de notre voisin."—" Le bien d'autrui ne nous est jamais nécessaire. Ce qui nous est véritablement nécessaire, c'est d'observer une exacte justice."—" La guerre est

NOTES

quelquefois nécessaire, il est vrai ; mais c'est la honte du genre humain qu'elle soit inévitable en certaines occasions."—" Quand les hommes veulent de la gloire, que ne la cherchent-ils dans l'application à faire du bien ? "—" Quoi donc ! une fausse gloire, un vain titre de conquérant qu'un prince veut acquérir, allume la guerre dans des pays immenses ! Ainsi un seul homme, donné au monde par la colère des dieux, sacrifie brutalement tant d'autres hommes à sa vanité : il faut que tout périsse, que tout nage dans le sang, que tout soit dévoré par les flammes, que tout ce qui échappe au fer et au feu ne puisse échapper à la faim, encore plus cruelle, afin qu'un seul homme, qui se joue de la nature humaine entière, trouve dans cette destruction générale son plaisir et sa gloire ! Quelle gloire monstrueuse ! Peut-on trop abhorrer et trop mépriser des hommes qui ont tellement oublié l'humanité ? Non, non : bien loin d'être des demi-dieux, ce ne sont pas même des hommes ; et ils doivent être en exécration à tous les siècles dont ils ont cru être admirés."

This last, eloquent, outspoken, and prophetic passage (*cf. Télémaque*, Bk. XIII,) was written in 1699, just a century before the Coup d'État of Napoleon the First, and shortly after the Treaty of Ryswick, the first of a long series of blows to the fortune, ambition, and prestige of Louis XIV, and an event which, together with the Revocation of the Edict of Nantes, marks the beginning of the disasters and humiliations of France. Well might Idomeneus-Louis XIV say on his deathbed—echoing, but too late, the sentiments of Mentor-Fénelon : " J'ai trop aimé la guerre, le faste, les bâtiments ; ne m'imitez pas en cela ! " *Cf.* Fénelon's *Lettre à Louis XIV*, p. 188, *supra*.

Note XXIV, to p. 62.—For the further elucidation of this chapter, the reader is referred to the interesting work of Gaston Bizos, *Fénelon éducateur* (1886).

FÉNELON

Note XXV, to p. **64**.—On Mme. Guyon, see her *Vie écrite par elle-même* (Cologne, 1740). In spite of the title, it is not probable that the work was written by her in its entirety ; it was no doubt compiled from the memoirs she had entrusted to Bossuet. The substance is certainly authentic. Consult also L. Guerrier's thesis, sustained before the Faculty of Letters of Paris : *Mme. Guyon, sa vie, sa doctrine et son influence* (1881). [Note by Janet.]

Note XXVI, to p. **64**.—Saint-Cyr was an educational and charitable establishment for poor girls of noble birth, founded by Mme. de Maintenon at the village of Saint-Cyr, a few miles from Versailles. The palatial buildings, constructed by Mansard, and splendidly furnished at a cost of 50,000 livres, were opened in 1686. In this *Maison d'Éducation*, which Saint-Marc Girardin has described as " la première sécularisation, sécularisation intelligente et hardie, de l'éducation des femmes," two hundred and fifty *pensionnaires* were boarded and educated gratis, from the age of seven to twenty, provided they could prove four degrees of nobility on the paternal side. The most admirable discipline prevailed in the School, which was conducted, on the whole, along the sanest lines, and according to the wisest methods. In the excellent Letters which she wrote to the mistresses and pupils, Mme. de Maintenon, who was a born teacher, offered judicious and practical advice on all manner of problems relating to religion, ethics, and social conduct. Saint-Simon, who had a profound dislike for her, nevertheless pays a tribute to the qualities of her style, which he characterises as " doux, juste en tous points, et naturellement éloquent et court." She constantly insists on sweetness of temper, gentleness, and frankness, as virtues essential to a charming woman, and one of her favourite maxims, uttered again and again in varying forms, is : " Soyez

raisonnables, ou vous serez malheureuses." But her
ideal is sober reason and sweet reasonableness, not
cantankerous reasoning, perverse quibbling, or cavilling
argumentativeness. The young ladies of Saint-Cyr
were trained to be neither " raisonneuses," nor " Précieuses," and Molière's lines, in the *Femmes Savantes*
(Act ii, Scene 7), could not have been applied fairly
to this *Maison :*

Raisonner est l'emploi de toute ma maison,

Et le raisonnement en bannit la raison.

Fénelon collaborated for a time in this work of education, writing mystic allocutions and spiritual directions
and instructions. Here, too, Mme. Guyon lectured
successfully on the disinterested love of God. But one
of the most noteworthy events in the history of the
School, was the performance by the pupils, in the presence of Louis XIV and Mme. de Maintenon, of Racine's
tragedy *Esther* (1689). The play—which contained
intentional or accidental allusions to several of the
most important personages of the day, *e.g.*, to the
former favourite Mme. de Montespan (*Vashti*), and to
Mme. de Maintenon (*Esther*) :

Sans doute on t'a conté la fameuse disgrâce

De l'altière Vashti dont j'occupe la place . . .

was performed more than a hundred times consecu-
tively. (*Cf.* Mme. de Sévigné, *Lettres* addressed to Mme.
de Grignan, Feb. 21 and 28, 1689 ; and Voltaire, *Siècle
de Louis XIV*, ch. xxvii.) *Athalie* (1691), described by
Voltaire as " le chef d'œuvre de l'esprit humain," was
also written for the girls of Saint-Cyr.

Mme. de Maintenon's foundation was destroyed at
the Revolution, and in 1808 Napoleon transferred his
military school from Fontainebleau to Saint-Cyr.

On Mme. de Maintenon and Saint-Cyr, consult :
Sainte-Beuve, *Causeries du lundi*, viii, xi ; O. Gréard,
Mme. de M. : Extraits de ses lettres, avis, entretiens et

FÉNELON

proverbes sur l'Éducation, précédés d'une Introduction (1884) ; *L'Éducation des femmes par les femmes* (1886) ; P. de Noailles, *Saint-Cyr : Histoire de la Maison Royale de Saint Louis* (1843) ; T. Lavallée, *Histoire de la Maison Royale de Saint-Cyr* (1853) ; P. Jacquinet, *M. de M. dans le monde et à Saint-Cyr* (1888) ; F. Brunetière, *Questions de critique* (1889) ; J. Bertaut, *La jeune fille dans la littérature française* (1911) ; G. Hanotaux et le comte O. d'Haussonville, *Souvenirs sur Mme. M. de M.* (1902) ; *Mme. de M. à Saint-Cyr ;* also Paul Janet, *Mme. de M. d'après* sa *correspondance authentique* in *Journal des Savants*, Feb. 1888.

Note XXVII, to p. 70.—A fashionable resort in Paris, created in 1616 by order of Marie de Médicis, whence the name *Cours la Reine*. It is an extensive avenue, running from the Place de la Concorde to the Pont de l'Alma, and lined with four rows of elms. The following lines, written in the eighteenth century, describe the various types of wasters, who habitually frequented the *Cours :*

> Les merveilleux, les petits-maîtres,
> Exhalant l'ambre le plus doux ;
> Les abbés, armés de lorgnettes ;
> Les robins aux cheveux flottants ;
> Les aimables impertinents,
> Et la foule de ces coquettes
> En lévite, en chapeaux galants,
> Ombragés de riches aigrettes,
> Qui cueillaient dans ces courts instants
> Le fruit de leurs longues toilettes.

Note XXVIII, to p. 71.—The only compromising document, in this connection, for Mme. Guyon is the letter which Father Lacombe wrote her from the Château de Vincennes, where he was imprisoned, and in which he says : " I admit in all sincerity that sin entered into certain things which took place too freely between us." (April 25, 1698 ; *cf. Œuvres* de Bossuet, xli, p. 194.) But Father Lacombe became insane a few months later, his testimony is, therefore, highly open to suspicion. [Note by Janet.]

Note XXIX, to p. 71.—This dangerous snare, into which certain mystics and occultists have fallen, through having been lulled into a sense of false security, and having forgotten to watch as well as pray, is alluded to by Boileau in his twelfth *Épître* (Sur l'amour de Dieu) :

C'est ainsi quelquefois qu'un indolent mystique,
Au milieu des péchés tranquille fanatique,
Du plus parfait amour pense avoir l'heureux don,
Et croit posséder Dieu dans les bras du démon.

As a matter of fact, such works as the *Spiritual Guide* (1675) of Molinos, and *Les Torrents* (1704) of Mme. Guyon, contain many perilously unguarded mystical propositions, which, like certain of the teachings of Labadie and others, have been perverted into the service of immorality.

Note XXX, to p. 73.—*Cf.* Bossuet, *Relation sur le Quiétisme* (*Œuvres*, xxvii, pp. 532-533.)—" *Corps,*" says Paul Janet, " here clearly signifies *corsage* or *corset*. It was not, therefore, merely a matter of the imagination, for Bossuet speaks further on of ' the bursting of her dress in two places.' " It was thus a case of real distension due to hysteria.

Hyperesthesia of the senses, especially of the muscular sense, often accompanies hysterical ecstasy. Even in those who have manifested various symptoms of this disorder of the nervous system in earlier years, this particular state of heightened muscular power is sometimes exaggerated by the imagination, labouring under the influence of a morbid religious auto-suggestion ; it is sometimes, though more rarely, entirely simulated.

FÉNELON

Dr. Paul Joire, in his *Précis théorique et pratique de Neuro-Hypnologie* (1892), says : " Quand les organes internes ne sont pas le siège de douleurs, ils sont souvent le point de départ de sensations perverties ou erronées qui sont purement subjectives. Les malades accusent des palpitations ou des pulsations artérielles qui n'existent pas ; elles se plaignent de ne pouvoir respirer, alors que l'examen direct démontre l'intégrité parfaite des organes ; elles font une énumération terrifiante des sensations extraordinaires qu'elles éprouvent dans l'estomac ou dans le ventre ; il n'est pas très rare que ces illusions viscérales coïncident avec des hallucinations sensorielles. Des contractures musculaires peuvent se joindre à ces sensations douloureuses et simuler diverses tumeurs à l'examen de gens peu exercés."

Note XXXI, to p. 74.—Dean Inge, in the Preface to his Bampton Lectures on *Christian Mysticism*, quotes the names of some typical mystics who were anything but unpractical dreamers. He writes : " As a matter of fact, all the great mystics have been energetic and influential, and their business capacity is specially noted in a curiously large number of cases. For instance, Plotinus was often in request as a guardian and trustee ; St. Bernard showed great gifts as an organiser ; St. Teresa, as a founder of Convents and administrator, gave evidence of extraordinary practical ability ; even St. Juan of the Cross displayed the same qualities ; John Smith was an excellent bursar of his college ; Fénelon ruled his diocese extremely well ; and Madame Guyon surprised those who had dealings with her by her great aptitude for affairs."

Note XXXII, to p. 77.—An allusion to the perverted views of family life expressed by Orgon, in Molière's *Tartuffe*. The hypocrite has so subtly indoctrinated Orgon that he takes the teaching of Matt. x, 35-37, quite literally. Thus Orgon (Act i, Scene 5),

referring to his friend Tartuffe, the *faux-dévot*, speaks
in the following terms to Cléante, his brother-in-law :
C'est un homme qui . . . ha ! . . . un homme . . .
    un homme enfin
Qui suit bien ses leçons, goûte une paix profonde,
Et comme du fumier regarde tout le monde.
Oui, je deviens tout autre avec son entretien ;
Il m'enseigne à n'avoir affection pour rien,
De toutes amitiés il détache mon âme ;
Et je verrais mourir frère, enfants, mère et femme,
Que je m'en soucierais autant que de cela !

    And again, in Act iii, Scene 7 :
Un bon et franc ami, que pour gendre je prends,
M'est bien plus cher que fils, que femme, et que parents.

    Paul Janet is thinking of one of the dangers inherent
in exaggerated Mysticism, *viz. :* the endeavour on the
part of certain mystics to " wind themselves too high
for mortal man," and thus to lose sight of the right
motive for personal sanctification (*cf.* John xvii, 19).
Mme. Guyon lacked the proportion and measure of true
faith, and, as Cléante, the embodiment of sanity in
religion, says, " une dévotion humaine et traitable."
Cf. Act i, Scene 5 :
    Et la plus noble chose ils la gâtent souvent
    Pour la vouloir outrer et pousser trop avant.

Note XXXIII, to p. 79.—" Tous ces faits de suggestion personnelle ou communiquée par une personne
étrangère, et se traduisant par des ecchymoses, des
hémorragies et des plaies comme dans les stigmatisa-
tions, *des guérisons subites* de folie ou de paralysie,
s'expliquent aujourd'hui tout autrement qu'on ne le
faisait jadis, et rentrent dans le domaine des expériences
que chacun peut faire sur *des sujets prédisposés au ner-
vosisme par l'hystérie* et l'hypnotisme."—" Les maux
engendrés par l'imagination exaltée, agissant par auto-
suggestion, ne sont rien en comparaison des bienfaits

qu'elle procure ; *ses guérisons sont innombrables*, et, quand elle ne guérit pas, elle apporte souvent l'espérance d'une amélioration prochaine. Souvent il suffit *d'avoir confiance* en celui qui peut guérir, pour être soulagé ou guéri. Les incubations dans les temples, les paroles magiques, les charmes, les talismans, les philtres, les amulettes, les attouchements d'un roi, d'un oracle, ou d'un magicien, les guérisons des homœopathes, en sont la preuve ; et les malades, qui croient fermement à ces influences et sont capables de se suggestionner, dans beaucoup de cas peuvent être guéris." (Dr. Paul Joire, *Précis théorique et pratique de Neuro-Hypnologie*, viii, pp. 223-225.) For a thoroughly exhaustive and authoritative scientific treatment of this subject, too long neglected in England, *cf.* Dr. Bernard Hollander, *Hypnotism and Suggestion* (1910). For a comprehensive study of Christian therapeutics, *cf.* Rev. Percy Dearmer, *Body and Soul* (1909). A classical work on psycho-therapeutics is Henri Bernheim's *Suggestive Therapeutics* (1886), English translation by Dr. C. A. Herter (1890). *Cf.* also Paul Janet, *Observations sur la suggestion hypnotique*, in Travaux Académiques, cxxii, p. 233 *et seq.*

Note XXXIV, to p. 82.—Their sublime, " la cime du grand," as Joubert calls it, *i.e.*, the highest, noblest, purest side of their nature. The word, which is in the singular in Saint-Simon, (*cf. Mémoires*, i, p. 177), is translated by the plural " sublimities," by Katharine Prescott Wormely, and " sublimes " by Bayle St. John.

Note XXXV, to p. 83.—The following is Saint-Simon's verdict on Fénelon's relations with Mme. Guyon : " Humanity blushed for him in regard to Mme. Guyon, for whom his admiration, real or feigned, lasted his lifetime, though his morals were never in the slightest degree suspected. He died a martyr to his admiration for her, for no one ever succeeded in separating him

NOTES

from it. In spite of the notorious falseness of her prophecies, she was always the centre round which revolved the little flock, and the oracle by which Fénelon lived and guided others."

Note XXXVI, to p. 85.—Contrast the case of the pious, but unlearned, Brittany domestic, Armelle (1606-1671), who served faithfully in one household during the thirty-five years of her life, edifying all who came in contact with her. Her life was written by the Ursuline Sister, Jane of the Nativity, and re-edited by the mystic Pierre Poiret, in 1704, under the title of *l'École du pur amour de Dieu ouverte aux savants et aux ignorants*. This little book is rendered all the more interesting from the fact that Poiret is also the editor of Mme. Guyon's *Poésies et cantiques spirituels*. There is an abridged life of Armelle in Duché de Vancy's *Histoires édifiantes*, written for the young ladies of Saint-Cyr.

Note XXXVII, to p. 92.—For a discussion of this point, and others raised in this chapter, as well as for an authoritative exposition of the speculations of the leading Quietists of the seventeenth century—Molinos, Mme. Guyon, and Fénelon, the reader should consult Dean Inge's Bampton Lectures (1899), on *Christian Mysticism*, Lecture vi, pp. 231-245. D'Alembert, in his *Éloge*, quotes a writer, possibly Bayle, as having said : " Je ne sais si Fénelon fut hérétique en assurant que Dieu mérite d'être aimé pour lui-même, mais je sais que Fénelon méritait d'être aimé ainsi."

Note XXXVIII, to p. 96.—A list of Mme. Guyon's works, with explanatory remarks, is given in the French edition of her Autobiography ; it is reproduced at the end of Thomas Upham's *Life, religious opinions, and experiences of Mme. Guyon*, the latest edition of which, with an Introduction by Dean Inge, was published in 1905.

FÉNELON

On this chapter and the next, the following works and critical studies should be referred to : F. Brunetière, *Études critiques sur l'histoire de la littérature française*, 2ᵉ série (1889) ; A. Bonnel, *La controverse de Bossuet et de Fénelon sur le Quiétisme* (1850) ; J. Matter, *Le Mysticisme en France au temps de Fénelon* (1864) ; A. Griveau, *Étude sur la condamnation du livre des Maximes des Saints* (1878) ; L. Guerrier, *Mme. Guyon, sa vie, sa doctrine* (1881) ; A. Le Roy, *La France et Rome de 1700 à 1715* (1892) ; A. Rébelliau, *Bossuet* (1903) ; L. Crouslé, *Fénelon et Bossuet* (1894) ; J. Michelet, *Du Prêtre, de la Femme, de la Famille* (1845) ; D'Alembert, *Éloges de Bossuet et de Fénelon ;* Voltaire, *Siècle de Louis XIV* (chap. xxxviii) ; on the psychology of Mysticism, *cf.* the Lecture given before the *Institut psychologique international*, in 1902, by Émile Boutroux. For a study of Mysticism, as a variety of religious experience, *cf.* William James' Gifford Lectures (1902).

Note XXXIX, to p. 108.—The publication of this book ought not to have taken place until after the one by Bossuet ; and Fénelon had made an express promise to this effect to the Archbishop of Paris. But his friends thought it necessary to hasten its publication, although Fénelon pretended he had no hand in the matter ; but we gather from his Correspondence that he was somewhat lacking in sincerity on this occasion, for he wrote to Abbé Tronson : " You see how important it is that my work should appear as early as possible." It was little tricks such as these, that caused Bossuet to say that M. de Cambrai was *un parfait hypocrite* (*cf.* Le Dieu, ii, p. 242). Far be it from us to use such expressions. It belongs to saints only to be so outspoken with each other. [Note by Janet.]

Note XL, to p. 110.—An exclamation which, in its French form, has become proverbial. It occurs in the

twelfth line of the First Canto of Boileau's *Lutrin*
(1672-1683) :

Mise, redis-moi donc quelle ardeur de vengeance
De ces hommes sacrés rompit l'intelligence,
Et troubla si longtemps deux célèbres rivaux :
Tant de fiel entre-t-il dans l'âme des dévots !

The last line—which, like the two preceding ones,
might be applied to the quarrel between Bossuet
and Fénelon—is an imitation of Virgil's well-known
epiphonema (*Aeneid*, i, 11) :

Tantæne animis cœlestibus iræ !

Note XLI, to p. 112.—Louis XIV, " le fils ainé et le
protecteur de l'Église," acting somewhat on the lines
of Henry VIII's ecclesiastical policy, had summoned a
National Council in 1681, with a view to the mainten-
ance of the provisions of the Concordat of 1516, and of
what were known as " the maxims, liberties, and privileges " of the Gallican Church.   The Assembly had been
presided over by Bossuet, who supported Louis XIV
in his protest against the encroachments of the Papacy
in temporal affairs.   Innocent XI annulled the decisions
of this National Council.   The reply of the Gallican
clergy, upholding the temporal independence of the
King of France and of the French Episcopate, was
expressed in the *Four Articles*, known as the Declaration
of 1682.

1. Saint Pierre et ses successeurs, et l'Église elle-
même, n'ont reçu de puissance de Dieu que sur les
choses spirituelles, et non sur les politiques et les
temporelles.

2. La pleine puissance spirituelle du Siège apostolique
et des successeurs de Pierre est telle que les décrets du
Saint Concile œcuménique de Constance, approuvés
par la Chaire apostolique (qui déclaraient les Conciles
généraux supérieurs au Pape en matière de foi),
subsistent dans toute leur force et vertu.

FÉNELON

3. De là résulte que l'usage de la puissance apostolique doit être réglé selon les Canons dictés par l'Esprit de Dieu ; que les règles, les mœurs et les constitutions reçues dans le royaume et dans l'Église Gallicane doivent rester en vigueur, et les bornes plantées par nos pères demeurer inébranlables.

4. Le souverain Pontife a la principale part dans les questions de foi, et ses décrets regardent toutes les Églises : cependant son jugement n'est point irréformable tant que le consentement de l'Église ne l'a point confirmé.

Cf. Matthieu Tabaraud, *Histoire critique de l'Assemblée du clergé de France en* 1682 (1826).

Note XLII, to p. 116.—The whole of this passage, which we quote from Cardinal de Bausset (ii, p. 124), consists of several extracts taken from different writings by Fénelon. The first : " When do you wish that we should end this business . . . ? " is taken from the answer to Bossuet's tract, *Schola in tuto* (*Œuvres complètes*, Édition de Saint-Sulpice, iii, p. 233).—The second : " You estimate and magnify . . ." is to be found in the Édition de Versailles, vi, p. 365.—The third: " We are, you and I . . . ," is taken from the *Lettre sur la réponse aux préjugés légitimes* (Édition de Saint-Sulpice, iii, p. 354). [Note by Janet.]

Note XLIII, to p. 127.—Jean Phélippeaux was for some time tutor to Bossuet's nephew. He represented Bossuet's interests in Rome, where he carried on secret negotiations. Later he was appointed Canon and Grand Vicar of Meaux. He wrote a most bitter and partisan book against Fénelon, published posthumously (1732), under the title : *Relation de l'origine, du progrès et de la condamnation du Quiétisme répandu en France, avec plusieurs anecdotes curieuses.*

Note XLIV, to p. 129.—It is this fact which, in our opinion, affords an explanation of certain passages in

NOTES

Fénelon's letters, which appear to conflict with the unconditional submission which he had shown at the time of the condemnation. For example, in a letter to Chanterac, he writes : " Nothing has really been decided in so far as the essence of the doctrine is concerned." In another letter, addressed to Father Le Tellier, we find this curious passage : " They have tolerated and ensured the triumph of the unworthy doctrine which degrades charity by reducing it to the sole motive of hope. *The one who was in error has prevailed ; the one who was free from error has been repelled.* God be praised ! " Have we not here a protest against the condemnation of his book ? No, for he adds : " *I attach no importance to my book, which I have sacrificed with joyful docility.*" All he means to convey, therefore, is that if his book deserved to be condemned because of certain verbal exaggerations, his doctrine had not been condemned in its essence ; and yet this is what was thought by " the King and the majority of people." That is why, according to public opinion, " the one who was in error had prevailed." Fénelon is therefore of opinion that people have drawn inferences from the Pope's decree, which were not implicitly contained in it. We might have had our suspicions, had Fénelon been alone to hold this view, but we are entitled to say that theologians of standing, such as Cardinal de Bausset, and the author of the excellent *Analyse de la controverse du Quiétisme*, in *Œuvres de Fénelon*, do not consider the doctrine of pure love to have been condemned by Rome (*cf.* Cardinal de Bausset, *Vie de Fénelon*, ii, n. xiv, p. 387, and *Œuvres*, iv, p. clxxxi). Fénelon himself expresses the same thought in a letter to Ramsay : " The Church, while condemning my book, has not condemned pure love ; this doctrine is taught in all the Catholic schools ; but the terms I made use of were unsuited to a dogmatic work." (Ramsay, p.

FÉNELON

155.) This also explains the *Mémoire pour être remis au Pape après ma mort*, referred to by Cardinal de Bausset (*Histoire de Fénelon*, ii, n. xiv, p. 383), some passages of which he quotes. In this document Fénelon expounded the theory of pure love, while still continuing to adhere to the Papal condemnation. Finally, the Gallican Church, as a whole, did not consider that pure love had been *ipso facto* involved in the condemnation of the *Maximes*, since, out of sixteen Metropolitan Assemblies, eight only, that is to say half, demanded the suppression of the apologetical writings : the other eight were therefore of opinion that the doctrine contained in these writings had not been condemned. (Bausset, ii, p. 291.) [Note by Janet.]

Note XLV, to p. 133.—For a further discussion of the fundamental difference in theological standpoint between Bossuet and Fénelon, and for fuller details concerning the various incidents in France, and the subterranean intrigues in Rome, which led up to Fénelon's condemnation, *cf.* R. Thamin, in Petit de Julleville's *Histoire de la Langue et de la Littérature française*, v, 8, pp. 465-475, and A. Rébelliau's *Bossuet*, ix, pp. 161-175.

Note XLVI, to p. 144.—*Cf.* Galatians v, 24 ; ii, 20 ; Romans vi, 6 ; vii, 24 ; Matthew xvi, 24.

Note XLVII, to p. 144—One of the best recent manuals on the subject is *L'Ange Conducteur des Ames Scrupuleuses* (1898), with a Preface by Canon Jules Didiot, of the Université Catholique de Lille.

Note XLVIII, to p. 148.—Andrew Michael Ramsay (1686-1743), a versatile *French* writer, and friend of Louis Racine and J. B. Rousseau. Besides his *Histoire de la Vie et des Ouvrages de Fénelon* (1723), an invaluable work, in spite of its being an apologia, rather than a biography, he also wrote : *Discours sur la poésie épique* (1717), often printed at the head of *Télémaque ; Essai philosophique sur le gouvernement civil selon les principes*

NOTES

de Fénelon (1721) ; *Voyages de Cyrus* (1727) ; *Histoire de Turenne* (1735), and other works, including a *Plan of Education*, in English, published posthumously. *Cf.* Pierre Sayous, *Le XVIIIᵉ siècle à l'étranger*, vol. ii, iv. 3 (1861).

Note XLIX, to p. **149**.—Pierre Poiret (1646-1719), the French theologian, and writer on Mysticism. Eugène Haag, the author of a masterly *Histoire des Dogmes*, says of him, in his *France protestante, ou Vie des protestants français* (1847-1859) : " Tous ceux qui le connurent s'accordent à louer son humilité et sa modestie, la pureté de ses mœurs, l'excellence de son cœur, sa bienveillance envers tous les hommes, sa modération, dont il ne s'écarta que dans sa polémique." He is the author of a large number of works of very unequal value ; he edited the Works of the visionary Antoinette Bourignon, in 21 vols. (1679-1684), and gave a new paraphrased translation of the *Quatre livres de l'Imitation de Jésus-Christ* (1683). *Cf.* Note xxxvi. *supra.*

Note L, to p. **150**.—The Savoyard Vicar's profession of faith is inserted in the Fourth Book of the *Émile. Cf.* John Morley, *Rousseau*, ii, 5, pp. 256-280.

Note LI, to p. **155**.—*Télémaque* appeared in 1699 owing to the indiscretion of a copyist, although it was written many years previously, in fragments, for the instruction and edification of the Duke of Burgundy. It is probable that no modern work has had more editions and translations, with the possible exception of Bunyan's *Pilgrim's Progress.*

The original manuscript contains no divisions, but Fénelon subsequently divided it into eighteen Books. The present writer possesses a *Télémaque Polyglotte* in six languages—French, English, German, Italian, Spanish, Portuguese—(1837) ; in this edition the work is divided into twenty-four Books.

The poetic prose style in which *Télémaque* is written

is generally condemned to-day ; its artificial descriptions, in particular, are anathema to teachers of good style. In this connection, *cf.* Antoine Albalat, *La formation du Style*, vii, pp. 139-151 ; Remy de Gourmont, *Esthétique de la langue française*, pp. 319-321 ; and, cautiously, Voltaire, *Mélanges littéraires : Connaissance des beautés et des défauts de la poésie.* On the other hand, Chateaubriand—whose prose poems, *Les Martyrs* (1809), and *Les Natchez* (1826), belong to the same type of composition—professes to have an open mind on the subject ; *cf.* latter half of the Preface to *Les Martyrs.* Writing on Fénelon, and his *Télémaque*, the bigoted Jansenist Abbé Barral says, in his notorious *Dictionnaire historique, littéraire et critique des hommes célèbres* (1759) : " He composed for the instruction of the Dukes of Burgundy, Anjou, and Berri, several works, among others the *Telemachus*, a singular book, which partakes at once of the character of a romance, and of a poem, and which substitutes a prosaic cadence for versification. . . . The fine moral maxims, which the author attributes to the Pagan divinities, are not well placed in their mouth. Is not this rendering homage to the demons of the great truths which we receive from the Gospel, and to despoil Jesus Christ, in order to render respectable the annihilated gods of Paganism ?—This Prelate was a wretched divine, more familiar with the light of profane authors than with that of the Fathers of the Church ! "

Note LII, to p. 163.—*Cf. Siècle de Louis XIV*, xxxii ; this chapter contains several inaccuracies as regards the *Télémaque ;* but elsewhere Voltaire says very finely : " On a de Fénelon cinquante-cinq ouvrages différents. Tous partent d'un cœur plein de vertu. Mais son *Télémaque* l'inspire." Voltaire looked upon the book as Fénelon's chef-d'œuvre.

Note LIII, to p. 168.—" Lorsque, délivré de ces affreuses peintures, il peut reposer sa douce imagination

sur la demeure des justes, alors on entend des sons que
la voix humaine n'a jamais égalés, et quelque chose de
céleste s'échappe de son âme : c'est l'extase de la charité
chrétienne enivrée de la joie qu'elle décrit. . . .
L'Elysée de Fénelon est une des créations du génie
moderne ; nulle part la langue française ne paraît plus
flexible et plus mélodieuse." (Villemain, *Mélanges*.)

Note LIV, to p. 169.—The substance of Fénelon's
instructions on the art of reigning was too radically
different from what Bossuet would have liked to have
imparted to the Duke of Burgundy, and the form " in-
sinuant et enveloppant " in which it was given in
Fénelon's Fables, and now in his " roman pédagogique,"
was too lacking in directness, for Bossuet either to have
commended the standpoint of this " réformateur chimé-
rique," or to have praised his *Télémaque*, a work which
Lamartine rather grandiloquently termed " l'évangile
de l'imagination moderne, qui fut classique en naissant,"
and which Émile Faguet refers to as " trop admiré
pendant deux siècles, trop décrié depuis, et qui reste un
des livres les plus originaux et les plus distingués de
notre littérature." F. Brunetière, whose judgments on
Fénelon, in his article in the Grande Encyclopédie, are
generally too severe, describes *Télémaque* as " une œuvre
d'une élégance et d'une distinction rare, unique en son
espèce, un peu au-dessous, mais pas très éloignée de la
tragédie de Racine." Villemain, an enthusiastic admirer, says : " Quoique la belle antiquité paraisse avoir
été moissonnée tout entière pour composer le *Télémaque*,
il reste à l'auteur quelque gloire d'invention, sans comp-
ter ce qu'il y a de créateur dans l'imitation de beautés
étrangères inimitables avant et après Fénelon. Rien
n'est plus beau que l'ordonnance du *Télémaque*, et l'on
ne trouve pas moins de grandeur dans l'idée générale
que de goût et de dextérité dans la réunion et le con-
traste des épisodes." D. Nisard sums up his judgment

on *Télémaque*, in the following words : " Cet idéal du simple, du naturel, de l'aimable, c'est là qu'il l'a réalisé. De tous les ouvrages écrits dans notre langue, celui-là est peut-être le plus aimable."

Note LV, to p. 176.—A complete and masterly study of the immortal Principles of 1789 will be found in *La Déclaration des Droits de l'Homme et du Citoyen* (Origines, discussions parlementaires, critiques), by Professor Alexis Bertrand. There is also a small but admirable Manual of civic and social education (1900) under the same title, written in collaboration with A. Belot, and published by Charles Delagrave, Paris. Both these books give the Text of the Seventeen Articles, which were drawn up by the Constituent Assembly, and which marked the culmination of the intellectual revolution prepared by Montesquieu, Voltaire, and the Encyclopædists. The Principles of this " Catéchisme national," or " Décalogue révolutionnaire," enshrine the democratic ideals of liberty and equality, the sovereignty of the people, the supremacy of law, the freedom of the press and of religious thought, the public control of the national exchequer, proportional taxation, and the security of private property. *Cf.* Paul Janet, *Philosophie de la Révolution française* (1874), and François Aulard, *Histoire politique de la Révolution française*, Third Edition, (1905).

Note LVI, to p. 176.—On Turgot (1727-1781), the political economist, and enlightened minister of finance under Louis XVI, many of whose wise reforms were carried out by the Constituent Assembly, *cf.* Alfred Neymarck, *Turgot et ses doctrines* (1885), Félix Rocquain, *L'Esprit révolutionnaire avant la Révolution* (1878), Taine, *L'Ancien Régime* (1875), and Léon Say, *Turgot* (1887), English translation by G. Masson (1888).

Note LVII, to p. 180.—Fénelon is the first genuine

NOTES

French Free Trader ; *cf. Plans de gouvernement*, xxii :
" Le commerce est comme certaines sources : si vous
voulez détourner leur cours, vous les faites tarir."

Note LVIII, to p. 183.—In place of Louis XIV's
dictum : " L'État, c'est moi ! " and of such monstrous
claims as : " Tous les biens des sujets appartiennent
au roi," Fénelon places before the heir presumptive the
true ideal which should inspire a constitutional monarch : " Un roi est fait pour ses sujets, et non les sujets
pour le roi."

Note LIX, to p. 184.—We have already seen Fénelon's
pacifist teaching in the *Dialogues des Morts*, and in
Télémaque, cf. Note xxiii. In his *Examen de conscience*,
he gives practical suggestions for the establishment of a
balance of power, or European Concert ; these, under
the circumstances, utopian views were revived a little
later by Abbé de Saint-Pierre, in his *Projet de paix per-
pétuelle* (1713), and *Discours sur la Polysynodie* (1718),
both of which were critically discussed by J. J. Rousseau
in his *Jugement* (1761).

Note LX, to p. 187.—Mme. de Maintenon does indeed
say : " Here is a Letter addressed to the King " ; but
it does not obviously follow from these words that the
Letter was handed to him. Moreover, Mme. de Maintenon adds that the Letter was written two or three
years before, which carries us back to the date mentioned above by the Marquis of Fénelon, that is to say
about 1688. But in that case, how comes it that the
Letter contains allusions to subsequent events ? [Note
by Janet.]

Note LXI, to p. 189.—Writing four years previously,
La Bruyère, in his *Caractères*, had drawn a harrowing
picture of the miserable condition of the masses of the
people : " L'on voit certains animaux farouches . . ."
(De l'Homme). *Cf.* also the political allusions in Racine's
Athalie, Act iv, Scene 3 : (Bientôt ils vous diront que

FÉNELON

les plus saintes lois . . .). ˙ *Cf.* De Tocqueville, *L'Ancien Régime et la Révolution*, ii, 12 ; iii, 5 ; also Fénelon's *Lettre à Louis XIV.*

Note LXII, to p. 194.—The Port-Royal edition of the *Pensées* (1670) was designedly incomplete ; *cf.* Émile Boutroux, *Pascal*, viii, and Lilian Rea, *The Enthusiasts of Port-Royal*, iv, 6, p. 314 (1912). The inaccuracies and mutilations were first pointed out by Victor Cousin in 1842. The best editions are those of Prosper Faugère (1844), and Ernest Havet (1852-1887).

Note LXIII, to p. 195.—This type of proof of the Existence of God, sometimes referred to as the teleological argument, is described in Professor A. Caldecott's *Philosophy of Religion* (1901), pp. 22-27, and discussed in A. C. Fraser's Gifford Lectures on the *Philosophy of Theism* (2nd edit., 1899), ii, 6, pp. 200-215. *Cf.* also Paul Janet's *Final Causes*, English translation, (2nd edit., 1883), with a Preface by R. Flint.

Note LXIV, to p. 202.—On Neo-Platonism, Plotinus, and his successors, *cf.* Alfred Fouillée, *Histoire de la Philosophie*, viii, pp. 159-176, and Victor Cousin, *Du Vrai, du Beau, et du Bien*, Leçon V (Du Mysticisme). A modified form of this mystical theism is to be found in the Cambridge Platonists ; *cf.* J. Tulloch, *Rational Theology in England in the Seventeenth Century* (1872), and Dean Inge, *Christian Mysticism*, vii, pp. 285-296.

Note LXV, to p. 211.—The best critical edition˜of the *Lettre à l'Académie* (1714), with an Introduction and Notes, is the one given by Albert Cahen (4th edit., 1908). Fénelon had been elected to the Academy in 1693, the same year as La Bruyère, and two years before his appointment to the Archbishopric of Cambrai. The Letter, says Raymond Thamin, was " le testament littéraire d'un survivant de la grande époque, . . . de l'exilé que l'Académie depuis seize ans n'avait pas revu."

NOTES

Note LXVI, to p. 213.—*Cf.* Matthew Arnold's essay on The Literary Influence of Academies, in *Essays in Criticism* (1st series, 1865).

Note LXVII, to p. 217.—In Racine's *Phèdre* (1677), Act v, Scene 6, beginning at the words :
A peine nous sortions des portes de Trézène. . . .

Note LXVIII, to p. 218.—This theory is expounded by Diderot in his *Paradoxe sur le Comédien* (1778).

Note LXIX, to p. 218.—The first Scene of the last Act of Corneille's *Cinna* (1640).

Note LXX, to p. 219.—Boileau appears to be the first to refer to *Athalie* as " le chef-d'œuvre de Racine " ; "*Athalie* est votre meilleur ouvrage," he says, " le public y reviendra." Voltaire called it " le chef-d'œuvre de l'esprit humain." La Harpe said every line was sublime, from the first to the last. Frederick the Great's admiration for this play was so great that he went as far as to say : " Je donnerais toutes mes victoires pour avoir fait *Athalie*." Victor Hugo, in his Preface to *Cromwell*, wrote : " Il y a surtout du génie dans cette prodigieuse *Athalie*, si haute et si simplement sublime, que le siècle royal ne l'a pu comprendre." *Cf.* Note xxvi, *supra*.

Note LXXI, to p. 220.—We have here another proof of Fénelon's courage and independence, for the profession of actor was still looked down upon by the ecclesiastical authorities. The priests of the Parish of Saint-Eustache had refused to attend Molière on his death-bed, and he had been " buried half clandestinely ; for the Archbishop of Paris, feeling perhaps that Molière's ethics were as irreconcilable with the received form of Christianity as ever those of Rabelais had been, forbade the clergy to say prayers for him." (B. W. Wells, *Modern French Literature*, ii, p. 79.) Moreover, Molière had not been admitted into the French Academy, although this body made tardy amends when, in 1778, it

287

FÉNELON

accepted a marble bust of Molière by Houdon, with an inscription by Saurin :

Rien ne manque à sa gloire, il manquait à la nôtre.

Molière was not the only truly " Immortal " writer who had the distinction of not occupying one of the forty Fauteuils of the Academy ; he is to be found, in this respect, in the goodly company of Descartes, Malebranche, Pascal, and La Rochefoucauld, in the seventeenth century ; Le Sage, Beaumarchais, Diderot, and J. J. Rousseau, in the eighteenth. *Cf.* Arsène Houssaye's interesting work entitled *Histoire du quarante et unième fauteuil de l'Académie Française* (1855).

Note LXXII, to p. 221.—In Boileau's second *Satire* (1664), addressed to Molière, lines 6 to 10.

Note LXXIII, to p. 221.—In La Bruyère's *Caractères* (1688), towards the middle of the chapter *Des ouvrages de l'esprit.*

Note LXXIV, to p. 222.—J. J. Rousseau's diatribe against Molière's *Misanthrope* is to be found in his Letter to D'Alembert *Sur les Spectacles* (1758), pp. 57-70 in Lucien Brunel's critical edition (4th, 1907). In thus denouncing the stage, on the score of its demoralising influence on actor and spectator alike, Rousseau is at one with Bossuet, Pascal, and the Jansenists.

Note LXXV, to p. 222.—In Boileau's *Art Poétique*, iii, lines 399-400—the last words of his qualified eulogy of Molière.

Note LXXVI, to p. 221.—The second Scene of the third Act of Molière's *Fourberies de Scapin* (1671).

Note LXXVII, to p. 222.—*Cf.* Professor Bury's inaugural lecture on " The Science of History," delivered before the University of Cambridge, in January, 1903.

Note LXXVIII, to p. 226.—Camille Jullian has written an admirable detailed survey of the French historians of the nineteenth century (1800-1896), in the 128 pages of the Introduction to his volume of

NOTES

Extraits des Historiens Français du xixe siècle (6th edition, 1910).

Note LXXIX, to p. 227.—This is Cato's definition of the orator. Quintilian likewise says : " Neque erit perfectus orator, nisi qui honeste dicere et sciet et audebit." (*Institutiones oratoriæ*, xii, 2) ; for there must be an essential congruity between the character of the orator and the aim which he sets before himself. Cicero has finely set forth what this aim should be : " Quidquid verum, utile, honestum est, quidquid ad religionem, resve publicas, scientias et artes pertinet . . . ut veritatem tueatur." (*Orator*, iv.) Hence Fénelon's beautiful adage : " L'homme digne d'être écouté est celui qui ne se sert de la parole que pour la pensée, et de la pensée que pour la vérité et la vertu."—" Rien n'est plus méprisable qu'un parleur de métier, qui fait de ses paroles ce qu'un charlatan fait de ses remèdes." (*Lettre à l'Académie*, iv.) So likewise La Bruyère in his *Caractères :* " Il y a des hommes saints, et dont le seul caractère est efficace pour la persuasion : ils paraissent, et tout un peuple qui doit les écouter est déjà ému et comme persuadé par leur présence ; le discours qu'ils vont prononcer fera le reste." (*De la chaire.*) " La principale partie de l'orateur, c'est la probité : sans elle il dégénère en déclamateur, il déguise ou il exagère les faits, il cite faux, il calomnie, il épouse la passion et les haines de ceux pour qui il parle ; et il est de la classe de ces avocats dont le proverbe dit qu'ils sont payés pour dire des injures." (*De quelques usages.*)

Note LXXX, to p. 227.—Janet is not only alluding to the abuse of Biblical quotations, but also, and especially, to the tactless habit of citing the classical writers of antiquity, and the Fathers of the Early Church, which had grown up since the Renaissance. As Raymond Thamin says : " On voyait Martial donner la réplique à Job, Aristote à Tertullien, Mucius Scevola figurer à

FÉNELON

côté de Saint Étienne, Régulus auprès de Jésus-Christ."
Cf. P. Jacquinet *Les Prédicateurs du XVIIᵉ siècle avant
Bossuet* (2nd edit., 1885).

Note LXXXI, to p. 230.—These ideas on simplicity
and unaffectedness, which figure so prominently in
Chapters IV and V of the Letter, and which are the
keynote of Fénelon, both as man and writer (*cf.* pp. 37, 38,
154, 167, 215, 217, 224, 231, *supra*), had already appeared
in Fénelon's *Discours de Réception à l'Académie* (1693) :
" Depuis que des hommes savants et judicieux ont re-
monté aux véritables règles, on n'abuse plus, comme on
le faisait autrefois, de l'esprit et de la parole ; on a pris
un genre d'écrire plus *simple*, plus naturel, plus court,
plus nerveux, plus précis. . . . Toute la perfection de
l'art consiste à imiter si naïvement la *simple* nature,
qu'on la prenne pour elle. . . . On a senti même de
nos jours que le style fleuri, quelque doux et quelque
agréable qu'il soit, ne peut jamais s'élever au-dessus du
genre médiocre, et que le vrai genre sublime, dédaignant
tous les ornements empruntés, ne se trouve que dans le
simple." Referring to Fénelon's style, Villemain says :
" Le style de Fénelon a toujours un caractère recon-
naissable de *simplicité*, de grâce et de douceur. . . .
Ce style n'est jamais celui d'un homme qui veut écrire,
c'est celui d'un homme possédé de la vérité, qui l'ex-
prime, comme il la sent, du fond de son âme." We are
reminded of Mme. de Genlis' fine saying : " La simplicité
n'est pas un mérite vulgaire : il faut en avoir beaucoup
pour avoir celui-là." *Cf.* A. Bourgoin, *Les maîtres de la
critique au XVIIᵉ siècle* (1887), and Abbé Urbain, *Les
premières rédactions de la Lettre à l'Académie* (1899).

Note LXXXII, to p. 239.—*Cf.* Letter of Abbé Tronson to Fénelon, March, 1698, *Correspondance*, ii, p. 381.

Note LXXXIII, to p. 240.—In spite of Saint-Simon's
testimony, we were already acquainted with the fact
that Fénelon's conduct towards the Jansenists was not

NOTES

generally judged so favourably. In order to obtain further light on this point, we had recourse to the kindly help of our colleague and friend M. Gazier, who is so deeply versed in the history of seventeenth and eighteenth century Jansenism. In answer to our request for information, we received the following letter, which he was kind enough to send us, and which we here reproduce in its entirety : " Saint-Simon is, as a rule, rather severe towards Fénelon ; he came very near making him one of his victims, as Sainte-Beuve says. Nevertheless, we read in his *Mémoires* (year 1711, after the death of His Royal Highness), that Fénelon, who was so opposed to Jansenism, and against which he had waged ' de grands combats de plume,' always allowed ' toute sorte de tranquillité aux Jansénistes, ou gens réputés tels,' of whom his diocese ' était plein.' This fact is all the more remarkable as, since the publication of some of his letters to Seignelay, Fénelon can no longer be held up as a model of toleration ; in this respect, as in many others, he belonged to his age. But these contradictions can be explained, if one takes the trouble to peruse his correspondence, and to collate letters which seem to have been scattered intentionally, and especially if one studies documents in record-offices, which relate to this affair, particularly the letters preserved in the archives of the Vatican. These letters, which were transferred to Paris by order of Napoleon, in 1810, were copied out in 1814 before being returned to Rome ; they shed an entirely new light on Fénelon's conduct. They prove conclusively that he exhibited a large measure of human frailty. As the irreconcilable enemy of those who had helped to bring about his condemnation, he desired to taste the delights of vengeance. First he endeavoured to obtain the anathematisation of the theologian Habert, the particular friend of Noailles ; next, he attacked, in conjunction with the

291

FÉNELON

Jesuits, whom Noailles had wounded to the core, the *Nouveau Testament* of the Oratorian Quesnel, published more than thirty years earlier, and which had repeatedly received the approval of Noailles, and had been defended by Bossuet. ' Silence within the Church,' says Saint-Simon, ' would have been the natural thing on the part of a Bishop, whose own doctrines had been solemnly condemned. He had too great wisdom not to perceive this, but he was filled with too much ambition. . . .' To ambition, he added a desire for vengeance. When the Bull *Unigenitus* appeared, Fénelon exclaimed : ' A hundred-and-one propositions condemned ! What a scandal for those who approved of such a book ! ' He requested that those who had given their approval should also be condemned, and he drove Noailles into his last retrenchments, storming against him in letters, in visit after visit, in memorandums, and even in open denunciations. So well had he manœuvred, that Louis XIV, formerly strongly prejudiced against him, was on the point of recalling him, when he died in January, 1715, on the eve of the consummation of his desires. For as the letters preserved in the Vatican clearly show, the King, in order to overcome the opposition of Noailles, was to summon a National Council for the purpose of excommunicating and deposing the Archbishop of Paris. The President of this Council was to have been Fénelon, who had accepted, and on whose behalf the purple was requested. This explains Louis XIV's exclamation on receiving the news of Fénelon's death : ' We shall miss him much upon occasion.' " [Note by Janet.]

Note LXXXIV, to p. 246.—*Cf*. Fénelon's lively and even playful account of the accident, in a letter written only six weeks before his death to his friend Destouches, in *Lettres et opuscules inédits de Fénelon* (1850).

Note LXXXV, to p. 255.—This unique document was first published by D'Alembert, who included it among the Notes (No. 5) appended to his *Éloge de Fénelon* (1774). D'Alembert adds : " Nous la donnons ici fidèlement transcrite sur l'original, qui est de la propre main de Fénelon ; on y remarque plusieurs ratures et corrections qui prouvent qu'il en était l'auteur. . . . Nous doutons qu'elle ait été présentée au roi, surtout par le duc de Beauvillier, qui n'y est pas trop bien traité." *Cf.* L. Crouslé, *Fénelon et Bossuet,* i (1894), and O. d'Haussonville, *La duchesse de Bourgogne,* i, p. 339 (1898) ; also pp. 185–191 *supra.*

APPENDIX I

Traité de l'Éducation des Filles, written in 1681, and published in 1687, in–12.

Traité du Ministère des Pasteurs, 1688, in–12.

Explication des Maximes des Saints, 1697, in–12. The best edition is the one published in Brussels in 1698.

All the controversial works dealing with the question of Quietism, and particularly Fénelon's answers or rejoinders to Bossuet, appeared in 1697 and 1698. An enumeration of them is to be found in the fourth volume of the Works of Fénelon (Versailles edition), in the Editor's Notice.

Aventures de Télémaque. After having granted his imprimatur, Louis XIV caused it to be suspended when the 208th page had been reached. This first edition (1699) bears the title, *Suite du IVe livre de l'Odyssée,* and comprised only four Books and a half. The same year the complete work appeared in five parts. In the subsequent editions, the division into Books was entirely arbitrary. In 1717, Fénelon's nephew gave an edition in twenty-four Books, with a Dissertation on epic poetry by Ramsay.

This served as a model for the innumerable editions which followed. The most noteworthy are Bosquillon's edition of 1799 (Year VII of the Republic), with the various readings, and the critical and historical notes of the preceding editions ; and Adry's (1811), the text of which is collated either with the manuscripts, or the best editions, together with a list of the critiques, satires, apologies, parodies, translations, and imitations of the work. There are countless foreign translations.

APPENDIX

Dialogues des Morts, 1714, in–12. The 1718 edition (2 vols.) given by Ramsay contains a greater number. The Dialogues between *Parrhasius and Paulius, Leonardo da Vinci and Poussin*, appeared in 1730, at the end of the Life of Mignard by Abbé de Mouville ; the remainder in 1787, in the quarto edition of Fénelon's works.

Dialogues sur l'Éloquence en général et sur celle de la Chaire en particulier, avec une Lettre à l'Académie française, published by Ramsay, in 1718, in–12.

Œuvres spirituelles (Antwerp, 2 vols. in–12, 1718, and Rouen, 1720, 4 vols. small in–12), including the *Lettres spirituelles*.

Examen de la conscience d'un roi, printed for the first time at the end of the Dutch *Télémaque*, 1734, reprinted in London and at the Hague, in 1747, in–12, under the title *Directions pour la conscience d'un roi*.

Lettres sur divers sujets concernant la Religion et la Métaphysique, 1718 ; there are five Letters.

Démonstration de l'Existence de Dieu tirée de la connaissance de la nature et proportionnée à la faible intelligence des plus simples, 1713, in–12, with a Preface by Father Tournemine, which was not sanctioned by Fénelon. A complete edition with the two parts appeared in 1718.

Recueils de sermons choisis sur différents sujets, 1710, in–12. These sermons are not all by Fénelon.

Essai sur le gouvernement civil, edited by Ramsay from Fénelon's conversations with the Pretender James iii (London, 1721).

COLLECTED WORKS

For a long time there existed no complete editions of Fénelon, although there were more or less complete collections of his works.

1. *Œuvres* de Fénelon, in nine volumes, in–4⁰, Paris, published by Didot, 1787-1792, edited by Abbé Gallard

APPENDIX

and Abbé de Querbeuf, with a Life of Fénelon by the latter.

2. Edition of 1810, in ten volumes, in–8⁰ or in–12.

3. Toulouse edition, in nineteen volumes ; more complete than the preceding editions, 1809-1811.

4. Besançon edition, in twenty-seven volumes, 1827, still incomplete.

5. Versailles edition, published by Lebel, 1820-1830. The Works are in twenty-two volumes, and the Correspondence in eleven.

6. Saint-Sulpice edition, in ten volumes, more complete than the preceding editions ; published by Leroux, Jouby, and Gaume, in Paris, 1851 and 1852.

ON THE LIFE AND CHARACTER OF FÉNELON

1. *Histoire de la Vie et des Ouvrages de Fénelon*, by Ramsay, London, 1723.

2. Abridgment of Ramsay's work by the Marquis of Fénelon.

3. *Vie de Fénelon* by Father Querbeuf, at the head of his edition of the *Œuvres*, 1787-1792.

4. *Histoire de Fénelon* by Cardinal de Bausset, 1808, three volumes, in–8⁰ ; 1827, four volumes, in–18. This Life figures at the head of the great Versailles edition.

APPENDIX II

THE serious student of Fénelon will need to consult Matthieu Tabaraud's *Supplément aux Histoires de Bossuet et de Fénelon*, 1822, and the *Histoire littéraire de Fénelon*, 1843, by Abbé Gosselin, who re-edited Cardinal de Bausset's *Histoire de Fénelon*, in 1850, and who, in 1851, in collaboration with Abbé Caron, gave a beautiful edition of the complete works of Fénelon, in ten volumes. Also the *Éloges* by D'Alembert, and La Harpe, and Sainte-Beuve's Articles in *Causeries du Lundi*, ii and x (1850 and 1854). F. Brunetière's Article in the Grande Encyclopédie should also be referred to, as well as Raymond Thamin's contribution to Petit de Julleville's *Histoire de la Langue et de la Littérature française*.

It is, of course, impossible to quote all the works on Fénelon, which have been written during the past 200 years. The following are a few of the most noteworthy recent studies in French : O. Gréard, *L'Éducation des femmes par les femmes* (1886) ; L. Boulvé, *De l'Hellénisme chez F.* (1897) ; A. Cahen, *Lettre à l'Académie* (1899) ; P. Bastier, *F. critique d'Art* (1903) ; G. Gidel, *La Politique de F.* (1906) ; A. Delplanque, *F. et la Doctrine de l'Amour pur, d'après sa Correspondance avec ses principaux amis* (1907) ; M. Cagnac, *F. Études critiques* (1910) ; J. Lemaître, *Fénelon* (1910) ; H. Brémond, *Apologie pour F.* (1910) ; A. Delplanque, *F. et ses amis* (1910) ; P. Sauvert, *F. Étude d'Ame* (1911) ; E. Griselle (Directeur de la *Revue Fénelon*), *F. Études historiques* (1911).

The following books, in English, may also be consulted : H. L. Farrer (afterwards Lear), *F. Archbishop of Cambrai* (1877) ; *Spiritual Thoughts for Busy People*, S.P.C.K. (1894) ; *Three Dialogues on Pulpit Eloquence*,

APPENDIX

translated by S. J. Eales (1896) ; E. K. Sanders, *F. His
friends and enemies* (1901) ; *Spiritual Counsels from the
Letters of F.*, selected by Lady Amabel Kerr, C.T.S.
(1904) ; *Letters and Reflections of F.*, edited by B. W.
Randolph (1906) ; S. H. Northcote (Viscount St. Cyres),
François de F. (1906) ; P. M. Masson, *F. and Mme. Guyon*
(1907) ; *F. Archbishop of Cambrai*, Extracts, (1908) ;
Meditations for a Month (1908) ; *The Maxims of the
Saints* (1908) ; *F.'s Maxims of the Mystics*, edited by
B. W. Randolph (1909) ; Darmesteter (A. M. F. Duclaux),
The French Ideal, Pascal, Fénelon, etc. (1911).

APPENDIX III

THE list of Paul Janet's works is a very long one; the following are among the most important:

LA FAMILLE, couronné par l'Académie française, 1855; 13th edition, 1890; translated into several languages.

LES CONFESSIONS DE SAINT AUGUSTIN, traduction française et une introduction, 1858.

HISTOIRE DE LA PHILOSOPHIE MORALE ET POLITIQUE DANS L'ANTIQUITÉ ET DANS LES TEMPS MODERNES, 2 vols., 1858, couronné par l'Académie des Sciences morales et politiques et par l'Académie française; 2nd edition, 1872, under the title *Histoire de la science politique dans ses rapports avec la morale;* 3rd edition, 1887.

LA PHILOSOPHIE DU BONHEUR, 1863, 5th edition, 1891.

LE MATÉRIALISME CONTEMPORAIN EN ALLEMAGNE, 1863, 5th edition, 1888; translated into several languages, into English by Gustave Masson, *The Materialism of the present day*, 1865.

LE CERVEAU ET LA PENSÉE, 1867.

ÉLÉMENTS DE MORALE, 1869, 4th edition, 1890; English translation by Mrs. C. R. Corson, *Elements of Morals*, 1884.

LES PROBLÈMES DU XIXᵉ SIÈCLE, 1872.

LA MORALE, 1874, 5th edition, 1898; English translation by Mary Chapman, *The Theory of Morals*, 1884.

PHILOSOPHIE DE LA RÉVOLUTION FRANÇAISE, 1874, 4th edition, 1892.

LES CAUSES FINALES, 1876, 2nd edition, 1883; English translation by William Affleck, with a Preface by R. Flint, *Final Causes*, 1878, 2nd edition, 1883.

APPENDIX

SPINOZA : DE DIEU, DE L'HOMME ET DE LA BÉATI-
TUDE, traduction française avec introduction, 1878.

LA PHILOSOPHIE FRANÇAISE CONTEMPORAINE, 1879.

TRAITÉ DE PHILOSOPHIE, 1880.

LES ORIGINES DU SOCIALISME CONTEMPORAIN, 1883.

LES MAÎTRES DE LA PENSÉE MODERNE, 1883.

VICTOR COUSIN ET SON ŒUVRE, 1885.

HISTOIRE DE LA PHILOSOPHIE, 1887, (with Gabriel
Séailles) ; English translation by Ada Monahan, edited
by Henry Jones, *A History of the Problems of Philosophy*,
1902, 2 vols.

LES PASSIONS ET LES CARACTÈRES DANS LA LITTÉRA-
TURE DU XVIIᵉ SIÈCLE, 1888.

HISTOIRE DE LA RÉVOLUTION FRANÇAISE, 1889.

LECTURES VARIÉES DE LITTÉRATURE ET DE MORALE,
1890.   (An excellent choice of Extracts made by Paul
Janet from his own works.)

LA PHILOSOPHIE DE LAMENNAIS, 1890.

FÉNELON, 1892.

PRINCIPES DE MÉTAPHYSIQUE ET DE PSYCHOLOGIE,
1897, 2 vols.

There are also a large number of smaller works, con-
sisting of Discours, Notices, Leçons d'ouverture, Cours,
Travaux académiques, Rapports, Articles in the *Revue
des Deux Mondes*, from 1856 to 1899, and in the *Journal
des Savants*, from 1888 to 1899, and Philosophical Reviews in *Le Temps*, from 1876, many of which are published in the *Comptes-rendus* of the Academy of Moral
and Political Sciences.

On Paul Janet, consult : Georges Picot *Paul Janet*,
Notice historique, lue en séance publique à l'Académie
des Sciences morales et politiques, le 6 Décembre, 1902 ;
Émile Boutroux *Notice* sur Paul Janet à l'École Normale ; and, for a critical review of his place in the
evolution of philosophical thought in France, Henri
Bergson's lengthy Article in the *Revue Philosophique* of

APPENDIX

November, 1897. Also the Articles in the Grand Dictionnaire Larousse, and the Article by Henri Marion in the Grande Encyclopédie. There is a poem entitled "L'Ame Immortelle," dedicated to Paul Janet, in Eugène Manuel's *Poésies complètes*, ii, p. 237.

APPENDIX IV

302

APPENDIX

submission, 126-7 ; Nisard's verdict on the case examined, 130-3 ; eminent qualities of Fénelon as a spiritual guide, 135 ; his directions to Mme. de Maintenon, 136-41 ; in particular, touching her influence with the King, 142 ; concerning family life, 143 ; the correspondence with Mme. de Montberon mainly concerned with the malady of scruples, 144-147 ; Andrew Ramsay's religious difficulties, 148-50, solved by Fénelon, 151 ; advice to Archbishop Colbert, 151 ; counsels to a military man, 152, to a young man at Court, 153-4 ; publication of *Télémaque*, its success, 155 ; comparison with the *Odyssey*, and the *Aeneid*, 156-59 ; finest episodes, 160 ; ethical purport of the work, 163 ; an indirect satire of the abuses of Louis XIV's reign, 164 ; its Christian inspiration, 165-6 ; qualities of its style, 167-8 ; contrasted with other great epics, 168 ; Bossuet's unjust opinion, 169 ; Fénelon's liberal attitude in political matters, 172 ; his democratic tendencies, 173-4 ; his practical politics exhibited in the *Tables de Chaulnes*, 175-6 ; favours a return to the States-General, 177 ; views on the relations of Church and State, 178-9 ; a free-trader, 180 ; conceptions of the duties of a King, 181-3 ; Fénelon, a pacifist, 184 ; his outspoken anonymous indictment of the King's policy, in his famous *Lettre à Louis XIV*, 185-91 ; his philosophical writings, 193 ; the most noteworthy is the *Traité de l'Existence de Dieu*, 194 ; analysis of the work, 195-202 ; his Neo-Platonist doctrine of the unity of God, described and discussed, 202-8 ; eloquent invocation to the Deity, 208 ; Fénelon, a critic of the first rank, his chief merits, 210 ; his *Lettre à l'Académie Française*, 211 ; views on language, 212, eloquence, 213, poetry, 214-5, tragedy, 216-8, comedy, 219, and Molière's plays, in particular, 220-2, history, 222-6 ; his opinions on pulpit oratory, 227-30 ; Fénelon exiled to Cambrai, 231, a typical day

APPENDIX

INDEX

305

INDEX

INDEX

INDEX